Fruits of Silence

Studies in the Art of Being

✿

HUGH L'ANSON FAUSSET

Abelard-Schuman

LONDON NEW YORK TORONTO

Contents

Preface

The first three chapters of this book were originally composed as addresses to different audiences, but the intervention of a serious illness prevented all but the first of them from being delivered. The last chapter in Part I was contributed as an article to *The Aryan Path*, but has been much enlarged. Part II has been written since I emerged from two years of extreme exhaustion, during which all my spiritual resources were put to the test, when in the long white nights I invoked the divine presence, as it seemed, in vain.

But looking back on that time of trial, I see now how necessary it was that my mind should have been silenced for a while by Silence itself. Even valid knowledge, if it has been gained on one level at the expense of others, can eventually stand in the way of further growth, though the impulse behind our search for truth may have been devoted and sincere.

Yet a man becomes distinctively human only when he begins to work on life with his mind and with a full awareness of what he is doing. He thus ceases gradually to be driftwood in the stream of change, and becomes sensitive to truths which have an eternal value and which he strives to incorporate in his existence. In doing so the flame of his spirit burns more brightly. For by opening himself to a timeless dimension, he finds in it not only the stable centre of his own being, but the power by which he can help to shape and transform the world about him. Consciousness is a door that will open eventually to a world of new being. But before that it is an ordeal which has to be endured, a fiery test by which the false in us is consumed and the truth unveiled. For man wakes slowly and for long his intelligence manifests only on the lower levels of his mind. On this level, governed by self-interest, we spin around us a mental cocoon in trying to meet the demands of life or to protect ourselves against a reality with which we feel ourselves as yet unready to cope.

Our brains, indeed, exist for this purpose, to step down the current of reality within the limits of our practical capacity. But too easily, hypnotized by habit, we come to assume that our spiritual capacity has the same narrow limits. So we cease to grow and the miracle of transformation, of breaking out of the chrysalis of mechanical thought and self-involved feeling, cannot occur.

But there is no dead-end to human consciousness as there is to animal sense. Mind may well seem in us at present no more than an ignorance striving ineffectually to know. But, like the heart, it is also a lens through which, when it is cleansed and pure, reality can shine. The spirit needs these faculties as the organs of its human expression and they need to be in harmony with one another. To become real, then, we have to discover that centre within and beyond ourselves in which they have a common root and creatively unite.

We shall not find it if we cling to a cosily human view of things. But we shall be even further from it if we lose our human bearings in a realm of abstractions. For reality transcends the thought or the feeling or the bodily sensations with which we habitually identify it and ourselves. And words are only of value in the degree that they lead us towards, or at best evoke, a condition in which all thoughts merge in a consciousness of being that shines by its own pure light.

PREFACE

This is the hidden treasure for which we all search in different ways and for which we have to go deep within, into that "secrecy", as the Indian sage, Sri Aurobindo, has put it, where the activity of mind is stilled. In and from that depth we shall not lose the world, but only our false view of it. For we shall hold there the golden key which frees us from our bondage and unlocks the door of communion with the whole of life. Understanding, where before we only knew by mental hearsay, and with a new awareness in which what we truly are will more and more inform what we do, we shall meet all pressures from within and without, firmly and flexibly.

This is a costly undertaking. But it can and should be a gay adventure too. It means abandoning all our habitual claims and defences and allowing the spirit to re-create us. For we are committing ourselves to something far more radical than moral improvement or psychological adjustment, necessary as these are. We are consenting to be changed in the very rhythm and texture of our being, to become quite other than we were. And how infinitely the reward will transcend the cost, as all that is partial in us is restored to the whole to which it belongs.

For by a constant effort of recollection, of reminding ourselves of that which we truly are and of renewing our readiness to live and die in it, we shall draw nearer to the moment when the unreal wound of division between body and spirit, self and not-self, is healed.

Such creative being and knowing may well seem at times an impossible ideal to realize. Yet if it is the truth to which all evolution tends, nothing can ultimately prevent its realization. Nor does it depend just on our own personal effort. For it is something in which we all share and not only here on earth. We are not just cogs in life's mechanism, but part of the evolving consciousness of man which we can advance or retard.

Moral reform, said Thoreau, consists in the effort to

awake and to stay awake. Whenever even a single soul awakes to its true nature, the light is quickened in other souls and creative forces are released upon which we can draw. If we look at the world today, we can hardly doubt that the time is ripe for such awakening and that mankind is now undergoing an evolutionary crisis of an unprecedented kind.

Can it achieve an inward development to match and illuminate the enormous extension of knowledge and power which the human mind has outwardly achieved? That is the only question which really matters. And the answer to it will depend on the readiness of each of us to labour to break down the walls of our habitual prison and so enter into a consciousness which not only knows, but creates, by its inherent love and insight, a new self and a new world.

In the silence of life at its lowest physical ebb I learnt something more of what that means and in Part II of this book I have tried to suggest from my own experience how we may set about breaking those walls down.

H. I'A. F.
Little Walden, Essex

PART ONE

✻

Spiritual Soundings

CHAPTER ONE

Reconceiving God

1

When I was first asked to speak on such an ultimate theme as the nature of the Divine and our relation to it, I felt how little right I had to suggest to anyone how he or she should conceive the inconceivable. For surely this is the one secret which each of us shares with his Maker and with no one else. Whatever we may try to say about that ultimate experience is, in the last resort, only a verbal reaction to something that is unsayable, something which only silence can compass.

Religious experience, on the other hand, is, in some measure, communicable, and since its quality and value to others depend entirely on the degree to which we are, in our own being, in touch with our creative source, our view of the nature of that source is of the first importance.

It is, of course, comparatively easy to discuss God and his attributes in theological terms. And perhaps the very name of God is so much out of favour today, except as an expletive, because it has so often sounded hollow on the lips of those who profess it. Nothing is more dead than a symbol which has lost its meaning and mystery. And how often today does the word "God" evoke a thrill of wonder and delight, of awe and devotion, a sense of solar glory and of the fathomless reaches of a great deep?

But symbols die that the reality behind them may be reborn. And the fact that the once vital God of Christian theology no longer quickens the imagination or satisfies the intelligence of many sincere seekers today, at least leaves a void out of which a new experience of what we call the divine may emerge.

For the fact is that theism itself in its traditional western form is in question. Certainly a modern Shelley would be unlikely to be sent down from Oxford for publishing a pamphlet entitled *The Necessity of Atheism*. Even in respectable religious circles it is now acknowledged that there are other atheisms than that of dialectical materialism, as there are other theisms than that of the Semitic faiths, and that a-theism does not necessarily imply the moral turpitude of the man or woman who professes it, as the Victorian believer liked to assume. After all, the first Christians were called "atheists".

Few modern atheists, outside Russia, are, in fact, the kind of scientific bigots so deliciously caricatured seventy years ago, in Mallock's *New Republic*, in the person of Mr Saunders, who declared that the eradication from the human race of any belief in God would afford an unending employment to all enlightened minds.

Our whole approach, in fact, is different. If we are to rediscover our source, we need to dig deep into ourselves as well as into the scriptures of mankind. For if man was created in the image of God, the God or Gods of his imagining throughout the ages have always reflected himself. The history of religion, as of the civilizations which religion has both nourished and warped, is the history of man's emerging and divided consciousness. No wonder that it is bloodstained. For man's God is as often his sin writ large and sanctified as the light of his being enthroned.

What men were at any given time, what were their dominant needs and fears, what stage in the long ascent from ignorance to true self-knowledge they had reached, were imaged in the divine figure or figures, whom they worshipped with ritual and sacrifice, and invested with an authority which it was a sin to disobey.

RECONCEIVING GOD

In the evolution of man's relation to the unseen Power which creates him we may note three stages. A medieval mystic, Joachim of Flora, divided prophetically the Christian dispensation into three epochs of progressive revelation of God to man, those of God the Father, God the Son and God the Spirit. Employing this symbolism for our own purposes, we may say that the epoch of the Father is that of primitive man whose God is the cosmic energy and will of which he is un-self-consciously aware. This God directs him through his instincts. He is the Lord of that lower realm of nature of which man is still intimately a part.

The epoch of the Son is that of man as he becomes self-conscious and imposes upon the universe a God in the likeness of himself. The righteous God who is the image and ideal of ethical and rational man aids him in controlling his animal appetites, but generally at the cost of suppressing or distorting his higher spiritual faculties. This, in fact, is the epoch in which man's unformulated unity with life is split into two and all the trouble begins.

The epoch of the Spirit is that in which divided man, through suffering and experiment and a profound change of mind, comes to realize that within himself, at his very heart, is a Being and a Consciousness which resolves the conflicts which have torn him asunder, and that this all-knowing and all-blissful Spirit is the Light within the Cosmic Power which, in the days of his innocence, before the serpent emerged in the garden of his mind, rocked him in the cradle of the natural world.

When men first began to think of this Cosmic Power, they saw it not as one, but as many. The mythology of polytheism reflected the various natural forces to which men were subject both in the world around them and in their instinctive impulses. The intimation that behind all these forces there existed a single integrating Power could only have occurred when they began to awaken to a sense of their own unique identity.

[15]

Each of us has known this moment in our childhood, when, in some sudden arrest of movement, some accidental or enforced separation from a familiar human setting, an anxious tremor shot through us. A first incredulous "Who am I? What is this world in which I move? Why am I here at all and why is *it*?" flashed across the virgin mind, a first intimation of the perilously strange situation in which the human creature is for long helplessly involved.

So it must have been with primitive man. And from this first question, oft repeated, there grew eventually a dawning realization that beyond the ocean of existence in which he was immersed there was a sublime Something which subsisted eternally in its own right, even before ever the forms of life appeared.

As the ancient Vedic hymn declared:

*Then there was neither Aught nor Nought, no air or
    sky beyond.
What covered all? Where rested all? In watery gulf
    profound?
Nor death was then, nor deathlessness, not change
    of night and day.
The One breathed calmly, self-sustained; nought else
    beyond it lay.*

It is from this dawning awareness of something that infinitely transcends our mental reach, and yet is the very essence of our being and of all existence, that every theism originally derives.

All man's speculation about God, all the poetry and worship, the sacrifice and defiance which he has offered him, is rooted in an intuition of Oneness, not an abstract conception, but a direct apprehension of the pure whole to which he belongs, a desire to preserve this wholeness or an anguished sense of having lost it and become alienated and alone.

It is in the epoch of the Son that this torment of division, of sin, as western moralists call it, becomes acute. Yet a distinctive human consciousness could not grow unless the reflective mind emerged in man to oppose the instinctive momentum of life. This untying of man as a unit of consciousness from his animal body and the body of nature is, we can see, a wholly necessary phase in his development.

Why, then, has this phase proved so disruptive to men, driving them to extremes of heroism and infamy, of elation and despair, and this despite the Oneness which envelops them and expresses itself as the persistence of a cosmos in which harmony overrules discord?

We cannot really say. We can only accept the fact that self-consciousness in man involves, as a condition of growth, an initial conflict, often fierce, between life and thought and all the opposites of which he and life are composed. Aspiration towards God is essentially an aspiration towards consciousness, which entails friction between different levels of the nature. Only so, it seems, can consciousness be generated and life regenerated. Yet the true purpose of religion has always been to resolve this conflict, to teach man, through the divine principle operating within him, to redeem the contraries in himself and so in his communion with his fellows and with the whole of life.

Men's Gods, then, are to be judged by the degree to which they embody this reconciling principle that pulses in the heart of life, and have inspired him to rise to a level of spiritual awareness and being, in which the sub-conscious depths and the super-conscious heights of his nature are re-united in the freedom of wisdom and love.

2

Man, however, cannot conceive truly the divine nature so long as he is inwardly divided. And it may help us to glance for a moment at two great fields of religious experience and see how this disease of dualism, as we may call it, infected their respective faiths.

First, then, what do we find in the Far East? The Aryan invaders brought to India (through their *rishis*) an imaginative faith which joyously affirmed the identity of the Cosmic Spirit and the spirit or real self in man, naming them Brahman and Atman. Brahman was at once transcendent Being and a creative consciousness which informed a universe that was an emanation of itself.

In appearance this universe was dual. But its duality was the play of an infinite intelligence which assumed such dual aspects as matter and spirit in the expansive joy of creation. All such opposites were but complementary modes of one informing Presence. From this Presence every appearance derived its meaning, derived, too, the part it played in the great cosmic drama of which the Brahman was at once the poet, the producer and the unseen actor.

But before the Aryans invaded the north of India, the indigenous Dravidian people had read the mystery differently. As they emerged from the primitive state, in which they identified themselves with natural life and its potencies, and so became increasingly conscious of the pains, hazards, and perplexities of earthly existence, they began to be troubled by a conjecture which was to haunt the human mind down the ages as it contemplated a world of sorrow and bondage so apparently hostile to the innate joy and the infinite needs of the spirit, as darkness may seem to be hostile to light.

Could it be, it came to be asked, that incarnation is a grievous fate thrust upon man, from which he should make every effort, short of suicide, to extricate himself and regain the immaculate realm of the spirit? Such was the dualistic doubt, the worm in the heart of the rose of the Dravidian earth-attachment, which, working in the obscure sub-soil of consciousness, challenged the creative faith of the Aryan sages, who declared that everything which lives, though clothed in matter, is essentially pure or, as William Blake put it, "holy". It is the interplay of these two views of life, the world-affirming and the world-denying, and of the practices which they dictated that has again and again renewed Indian thought and driven her forward on her tireless spiritual quest.

I may add just this. Hinduism and Buddhism enthrone as the source and goal of the religious quest, not a personal God as ordinarily conceived in the West, but a supreme unconditioned Consciousness in which man's own consciousness is meant to find its freedom and its peace. To the Vedantist the idea of a personal God as a magnified individual, like man in His nature, but greater and vaster, is a vulgar notion, which encourages all too easily ideas of currying favour with God or buying off his anger.

Brahman, indeed, is no impersonal abstraction or he could not inform concrete realities and personal activities. And though he exceeds the bounds of any sense-object, he may be worshipped under various forms, which image aspects of his creative Selfhood, or in the person of a divinely endowed teacher, such as Krishna. But Brahman ever transcends the forms, bright and dark, in which he manifests and in which he is ever undivided.

Always, for the aspiring Indian spirit, beyond any humanly definable God is an infinite Consciousness that creates, no static Absolute, but an ineffable Lord of Being, who lives in the birth, growth and dissolution of all things, yet is changeless; who, if named as a concession and aid to the human mind, is in essence unutterable, and who can be truly known only by those who rejoice that he is unknowable.

How alien, then, to the Indian *rishi* or the Chinese sage is the jealous and joyless God whom parts of the Old Testament so largely imposed upon the Christianity of the West, despite the transforming genius of Jesus and the

[19]

insight of such Christian mystics as Dionysius, Eckhardt and Aquinas, who never forgot the Godhead in the God. The august Almighty who dominated the Semitic imagination does indeed represent man's moral situation when he first awakes to his condition as an erring, self-conscious being. Yet in the Jehovah of the Pentateuch we see much of the fear-ridden ego which primitive man projected into the heavens above him. Against this celestial super-ego a part of him inevitably rebelled. But before it another part bowed down in guilt and contrition.

The God of the Jewish, as of the Islamic faith, is, in his exoteric guise, an authoritarian ruler who proclaims his law through the mouths of his prophets and sternly punishes transgressors of it. He is conceived as imposing his will upon man and nature from outside, which has encouraged western man to impose his will in like manner upon his natural and human dependents, often for their supposedly moral good.

In the West the Judaic dualism was resolved in the person and teaching of Jesus, who declared that he and the Father were one, even as the Eastern Masters had declared that Brahman and Atman were one, and who, in his life and death, revealed how the divine power and intelligence, working in man, could redeem the warfare of the contraries from a newly-found centre of being. In him the God of nature and of penal law became a God of love, who awakes in the heart of those who transcend what T. E. Lawrence called "that diseased antithesis of flesh and spirit" which underlies the fever and frustration of an unregenerate world.

Nevertheless, for very many, the God of the West, for all the transcendent grandeur of Hebrew prophetic monotheism, has remained predominantly a super-human ruler of a one-sidedly masculine type, as the militant history of the Christian Church shows, as well as the emphasis which Protestantism, in particular, has laid upon moral discipline at the expense of metaphysical or psychological truth. It is significant, too, that the traditional conception of man as a trinity of body, soul and spirit, was changed by ecclesiastical decree in the ninth century.* Henceforward man was to be regarded as a duality of body and soul, though the soul was allowed some spiritual faculties. Thus the spirit, as the creative principle within man which orders and harmonizes his dual nature, was largely externalized. To that extent man was diminished as a spiritual being, and God exalted as an outside power.

Despite all this, countless Christians, of course, have lived the imaginative truth of Jesus's teaching. For behind the dualistic view which draws its strength from the lower levels of man's nature, whether expressed positively in the West or negatively in the East, there lies deep in man a conviction that the Cosmos is one and that he is one with it, that the division into which he has fallen in becoming self-conscious is unreal, despite the terrible evidence of it in the life around him; that it is a wound which he has received or inflicted on himself, and that this wound can be healed.

3

Now what is the relevance of all this to our own immediate situation? Man, we have seen, may misconceive God in two ways.

He may be so intensely conscious of his divided condition that he longs to escape from the confines of matter and the pains and hazards of human development and be resumed in his unseen essence. The God of his desire will then be pure spirit, calm, silent and uninvolved.

On the other hand he may be so resolutely contained within the bounds of himself that, in one way or another,

* At the Eighth Oecumenical Council held in Constantinople in A.D. 869.

he will project the bias of his partial selfhood into the creative power which he worships and which he invokes to reinforce his own desires and purposes. His God will then be, more often than not, a combative, righteous God, opposed to Satan and all his works.

Today most intelligent people rightly reject both these one-sided conceptions of God, but too often without finding any satisfying alternative. Yet without an integral conception of what we really are we cannot recover the divine rhythm which consists in being at once perfectly tranquil in soul and lovingly decisive in action. Such creative living springs from a realization of God as at once the unconditioned spirit which transcends the life of time and the imaginative will and energy which, moment by moment, inform it.

To live then in the likeness of God involves wholly accepting existence, with all its apparent blemishes, but in such a way that we are no longer bound by it or to it. What binds us to existence is the self-centred mentality which perverts equally the life of instinct and the light of understanding.

Can, then, the traditional theism of the West and the creeds associated with it deliver us from such self-consciousness into wholeness of being and doing?

Fifty years ago, in the famous Gifford lectures, later published under the title *Varieties of Religious Experience*, William James showed how impotent dogmatic theology often is to liberate the spirit or help people to live. The religious experiences which he recorded went far to prove his conclusion that the visible world is part of a more spiritual universe from which it draws its significance. But he had to admit that those who claimed to have been converted, and particularly, perhaps, the Biblical zealots among them, failed often, in their lives and persons, to show the qualities to be expected of the "supernaturally saved".

There is, as we know, all the difference between an

emotional or even mental expansion of the self and its real enlightenment. To awake to the light of a new awareness we need, indeed, to break out of our mental prison. But we shall not do this by a rush of feeling or by merely modifying our thoughts about God, still less by "waiting for Godot" in the sense of just hanging ruefully around. We need, rather, to provide the conditions in ourselves by which we can be recreated in the likeness of what we really are. For we cannot truly reconceive God unless we allow God to reconceive us.

"If the soul is to know God," Eckhardt declared, "it must forget itself and lose itself." But can it fearlessly forget itself in relation to a God regarded as an almighty moral overseer? Should not, then, our first concern be rather to commit ourselves to That which is beyond our power to define, but from the mysterious depths of which true images of the divine may arise to enlighten the dedicated mind? Is not surrender to this "Nothing", as the mystics call it, this ego-less Void in which all IS, the ultimately necessary act of faith, and not belief in or attachment to the formulated God of the theologians? To make this surrender is not to flee the self or disclaim the guilt in which each of us, through self-love, is involved. But it is to open ourselves, responsibly, to a dimension from which alone the guilt of our greed or our righteousness can be redeemed and in which the necessary props of doctrine and morality cease to fortify the ego and support instead the growing soul.

It is by such a basic commitment, so much more costly and comprehensive than the mere social involvement, which is the catchword of the moment, that the true artist conceives and creates. And though it may well seem arrogant to compare our small moments of relatively integrated experience with that of Bach composing his great B Minor Mass, or of Michaelangelo at work on the ceiling of the Sistine Chapel, yet we could not identify ourselves with the art of the Masters if we did not possess within ourselves the potentiality for such imaginative acts and the capacity to perform them within the far smaller range of our own endowments.

It would seem that authentic religious experience, on whatever level or in whatever medium it manifests, is distinct from all other experience in this – that, in different degrees, it engages and harmonizes all our faculties of thinking, feeling and willing, and so, for the time at least, helps us to realize what it is to be whole. In fact we awake to the mental and moral life of self-consciousness for no other purpose than that it should lead us out of the automatism of instinct and blind feeling, and then beyond itself into the freedom of such at-onement. To live wholly within and beyond ourselves in what we do and are is, in the light of such moments, beyond any argument, to fulfil our human destiny on earth. It is only, then, in our purest creative moments that we can approach a true apprehension of the nature and being of God. All conceptions of him, however revered by tradition or linked with ecclesiastical usage, which fail to accord with this, reflect impure acts of the human mind and imagination.

Such an obvious act is that which projects man's own conflict into God, appealing to him to take sides in the struggle which man, for a time, must wage between the subconscious forces in his nature which he calls Evil and the super-conscious and ultimately liberating forces which he calls Good. In such a willed warfare God can at best be only partially known. For our bodily instincts are just as rooted in reality as our spiritual passion for the true, the good, and the beautiful. Admittedly the conflict in unregenerate life cannot be evaded. The first condition of entering the field of the higher intelligence and seeing Truth face to face is, as Dr. Jasink has said in one of his lectures, "that a man should purify his physical, psychic and mental bodies by moral discipline."

Every true teacher of the Way has said the same. But it is

[24]

by charity, humility and attentiveness, by what Simone Weil called *"l'attente de Dieu"*, that we can invoke the grace and power of the Light, and not by looking to God as our great commander in a campaign for moral betterment. For such a God only impersonates our delusion that we ourselves can will the good and the true. And until we have outgrown that delusion, we cannot learn the secret of the effortless act, the act of the enlightened will. Morality, alas, so often divides, through being *self*-willed. But a truly moral act fulfils the deepest needs of human nature by uniting it with that will at the heart of things of which Wordsworth wrote:

> *Thou dost preserve the stars from wrong;*
> *And the most ancient heavens, through Thee,*
> *are fresh and strong.*

Thus, too, direct insight into reality comes, not by painfully striving after enlightenment or by acquiring ideas and beliefs, but by consciously participating in the Universe as a living, intimately related whole, and so in the work of creation. True goodness is nothing less than this.

Perhaps, then, the contemporary tendency to "leave God out of it, shall we?" is not quite so godless as respectable moralists suppose. It may, at least, betray a healthy instinct against using God as a mask for our own dubiously dutiful or devious designs.

Yet the need persists in many to worship God in the likeness of man. Nor is this need in itself illicit, since the Creator has clearly chosen man to be, in the human order, a mirror of himself and dwells in his heart so that man may eventually come to realize, through and beyond his personality, that one highest Self of all.

Yet any human or mythical figure, even those who touch our hearts and satisfy our minds most deeply, a Krishna, a Christ, or a Buddha, is only a form, however perfect in its kind and rich in meaning and inspiration, of That which surpasses every image in which It reveals and conceals Its mystery.

Only in a mind that neither idolizes nor appropriates the divine by clinging to it, and so is a vessel able to receive the truth wherever it manifests, can the creative spirit renew itself from moment to moment, growing ever more real and present in the evolving soul. This is the miracle of divine incarnation which is waiting to reveal itself to us on every level of life. The idea of God, as John Scotus Erigena said, breaks differently through the prism of different personalities. But any idea or image of Him which does not spring, uncorrupted by what we want or wish, from that primal fount of life and light, of which the mystics and sages speak, will bind us to that part of ourselves which it reflects.

If, then, today we are to recover the ability to experience God as the creative principle of our being, many of us need, I think, to go beyond the theism and the a-theism which have fought or disdained each other in the past and especially in this scientific era.

If we can abandon altogether the arguments and counter-arguments, in which our restless minds take so painful a pleasure, and so become still and alert to reality, we shall find a deeper faculty of knowledge opening in us, that "Golden Flower" of intuitive awareness, in which the conflict of doubt and belief, characteristic of the mental selfhood, is resolved and the true polarity established.

Admittedly many of us will still need to fight the conflict out until we are convinced of its futility. For we have still to experience, beyond question, the reality of that true reason of our being which resolves it. In other words we have still to prove the truth of that simple, pregnant, but too often sentimentalized saying, "God is love". For love is the power which, unbound and unbiased itself, binds up, through its reconciling genius, what we in ignorance break in two. In everything it restores the true pattern.

RECONCEIVING GOD

Those who like to think of God as a person may complain that to conceive of him as the forever hidden third term in the conflict of life is to provide nothing for mind and heart to hold on to. But surely that is, ultimately, just what is needed, if the divisive grip of the ego is to be loosened and we are to find our true centre in a Consciousness and Being which is not one-sidedly personal, but which includes the "I" and the "not-I" in Itself and so makes possible that true communion with life, within and without, which at once fulfils and extinguishes all our partial desires.

For the disinterestedness which the scientist practises in his physical experiments is just as necessary, but much more difficult, in the field of spiritual experience, if we are not to do violence to Truth. Disinterestedness is the one sure proof of faith. Without it we are still clinging to our private defences and preferences, however fervently we may profess our belief.

To return, then, to the symbolism which I used earlier, the Epoch of the Spirit, which I believe is opening before us in this age, with possibilities of newly integrated life and consciousness, does not contradict or supersede the epochs of the Father and the Son. Rather it completes and comprehends them. May not that be the deeper meaning of Jesus's words – "It is expedient for you that I go away: for if I go not away, the Paraclete will not come unto you."

Man will not cease to see God in the image of human perfection and as the great original of what he knows himself potentially to be. For truly "the Masterpiece is of ourselves as we are of the Masterpiece". Nor will he cease to experience God in the majestic order and illimitable power of the cosmos and in all those voices, stern or caressing, with which Nature speaks to soul and sense.

But in the universe and all its evolving forms he will see the play of that divine Oneness which is the key-note of his own being and which impels him ever to exceed the negative bounds of himself.

FRUITS OF SILENCE

A mental assent to this Oneness is not enough, nor a sentimental abandonment to it. We are called to engage in what Traherne called "a work of unspeakable diligence and an argument of infinite love", recollecting ourselves in such a way as to forget ourselves in That which, moment by moment, recreates us as unique expressions of Itself. It is in this recollection, infused into what we think and feel and do, that the craft of the contemplative life consists. By it we may begin to learn the measure and the meaning of the divine. This ever more sensitive and imaginative embodiment of the divine in our being is the greatest and most difficult art of all.

A God who divides, however awesome and authoritative, is but an image of fallen man. The God who unites exceeds man's mental reach, but he is directly experienced when body and soul, heart and mind consent to be at one in That of which the seer of the Upanishad declared:

Him have I known, the Great Spirit,
Him who is Light, who is beyond darkness.
To know Him, and Him alone, is to pass beyond
  death –
There is no other way.
He is the whole, other than He is naught,
Greater or smaller there is nothing other.
Still as a tree, unshaken in the heavens,
His living Being fills the Universe.

SWETASWATARA UPANISHAD

✿

CHAPTER TWO

Yoga and Jung

1

In our journey through life we move, inwardly as well as outwardly, between the light and the dark. A sunlit, if often clouded, sky over-arches us and we voyage over sightless waters through which glide the monsters of the deep. This height and this depth contain within them the dual poles which keep our being in balance according as we respond, from a stable centre, to their positive and negative pull.

But mostly how faulty our response is! We sink or plunge into the dark or we grasp avidly at the light, swayed by one-sided impulses. The height to which we unconsciously aspire is the lucid realm of pure spirit, in which truth, uncontaminated by gross matter, reveals its ideal forms. But the depths in which we are physically rooted are the realm of sentient soul, in which the creative idea that we are meant to embody is hidden as a seed in the womb of life, evolving in time towards a realization of its true form.

For long we do not see the abyss at our feet or suspect the potential danger of the solar radiance which reaches us, mercifully, through thick veils of carnal ignorance. So long as consciousness sleeps within our flesh, we are insured against all inward hazards. And even when it awakes in an ego which seeks its own satisfactions and tries to impose its own partial will upon life, self-consciousness is far from being a painful or perilous condition for many people.

[29]

Indeed, since the human world about us, in which self-interest and material satisfactions are the controlling motives, reflects just such a condition, those who live the ego-centric life in its more agreeable forms may well seem better adapted to their environment than those who are in incipient revolt against it.

Yet consciousness, centred in the ego, as it must be when we first awake from the sleep of nature, manifests as tension between feeling and thought, the feminine and masculine modes of our being. It can be a creative tension, as in an intimate and mutually educative love-relationship. But unless there is a persisting will to resolve the element of conflict latent in the ego by relating ourselves to some principle which transcends the opposites, the tension will cease to serve a creative purpose and ultimately impose such a strain upon the personality that it breaks in two.

> *Things fall apart; the centre cannot hold.*
> *Mere anarchy is loosed upon the world. . . .*

It is an anarchy in which the individual swings helplessly between the powers of the abyss and of the height. And anyone who has witnessed the terrible impotence of a psychotic will not question the reality of those powers.

This is, of course, the pathological extreme into which an ego-centric life can collapse under unbearable strain. But along this hazardous razor-edge we all, as evolving souls, journey, for the most part ignorant of its dangers until some crisis in ourselves or our world shocks us into appalled awareness.

The purpose of all the great teachers and of the religions which have derived from them has been so to guide us on our journey that we shall avoid catastrophe by learning in time what we truly are. Doubtless many people live the self-centred life in a diluted form, as immune to psychic disaster as to high spiritual achievement. Certainly in our material civilization this kind of low-toned life of mediocre aims and trivial satisfactions, of respectable selfishness, has become almost the norm. Such a life may provoke no crises, but it deadens the deeper impulses of growth and chokes the spring of vitality which should quicken in us the need ever to exceed what at the moment we are.

Nevertheless the need cannot be stifled indefinitely and there are many today, even among those who have outwardly adapted themselves with fair success to their environment, who find a life of secular compromise more and more deadly and begin to thirst for a reality with which they have lost touch. To find this reality it is not enough merely to associate with others in public worship or in laudable social activities. To satisfy it, it is necessary to enter upon a path of self-enquiry, self-adjustment and self-discovery.

In this brief paper I am concerned only with two branches of this path which are attracting today persons who cannot subscribe to some of the tenets of orthodox Christian belief. To the first of these I give the name of *Yoga*, but only in a wide sense, as representing one mode of a method of self-release which has been immemorially practised. The other is "depth psychology", the modern technique of analysis and integration, based upon the teaching of C. G. Jung. It is with the implications of this technique that I am concerned and not with the vast mythological and alchemical learning of the Master. At the risk of being thought an ignorant outsider by initiates of the Jungian mysteries, I want briefly to consider these two methods, not as rivals, but as, in some measure, complementing each other.

2

Yoga and "depth psychology" are alike concerned to restore the human consciousness to its true centre. To achieve this the psychologist focuses attention upon what lies beneath self-consciousness, upon man's ancestral heritage, his psychic past, the primordial landscape of the human mind. For deep within each of us, at the very roots of our being, is an immense ocean of primitive life from which our distinctive humanity has emerged. In struggling out of the primeval ignorance of this realm of instinct man has acquired a store of invaluable experience, much of which lies hidden when our minds are awake but can, in part at least, be recovered when we sleep and dream. This is the realm of what Jung has called the "collective unconscious". And his therapy is based upon it.

By contrast the seer of the traditional teaching directs the attention of his pupils and disciples primarily to the metaphysical realm, the realm of pure knowing and being, from which, it is held, man, in his essentially spiritual essence, descends, as indeed do all the forms of manifested life. I need hardly say that such words as "above" and "below" in this context are only metaphors drawn from space to suggest different planes of reality within us, with which planes of the outer world crudely correspond. Metaphorically that which lies beyond the grasp of our self-conscious minds can be likened to a sphere or circle within which we are each groping for the centre. Like space itself as experienced by us who dwell on a rotating planet, this sphere has an upper and a lower hemisphere.

The seer teaches that salvation comes from above. "Except a man be born again from above he cannot enter the Kingdom of God." In other words the self-centred individual needs to invoke consciously the light that descends from this higher or more interior plane to redeem the instinctual forces which rule his earth-bound nature. The methods of prayer, contemplation, devotion and worship are all directed to this end. Doubtless they have often been misused or negatively opposed to the instincts which they are meant to purify. But any technique of integration which disregards them must, it would seem, achieve only a limited enlightenment.

Yet despite Jung's repudiation of metaphysical ideas as unverifiable, it would be absurd to suggest that he denies metaphysical reality. For that is to be found in the depths as well as in the heights. But in the subconscious depths the perfect light and power and beauty of the supreme consciousness, as we apprehend it in our purest moments, is involved in the obscurity of dense matter and terrestrial being.

The whole of the traditional teaching springs from and is an application of a vision of such a supreme consciousness, as the transcendent heart of Creation. This Absolute of knowing, being and bliss is conceived as condensing in the first stage of its devolution into a Creative Power or Person, though the word person is quite inadequate to express the limitless nature of the divine Originator, whether we call Him God or Ishvara. Within the original unity of this Lord of the Cosmos two principles exist, the one positive, the other negative. The positive principle is spirit or pure consciousness, the negative is primordial substance or pure potentiality. In human terms we may call the one the engendering Father, the other the Virgin Mother. Through their union the entire universe of forms is born and re-born. As creation proceeds and spirit incarnates at deeper and denser levels of its opposite, the original substance of life eventually assumes the nature of the inanimate matter which is the basis of the physical world.

In the traditional teaching man as an essentially spiritual being descends, too, from God, his source, into the darkness of matter. Like the cosmos, he is born of water and of the spirit. And hidden in the psychic centre behind his heart lies a seed of infinite reality, the jewel within the lotus, which is the inmost truth of his being. But of this every child of man is born unconscious. And when a distinctively human consciousness first glimmers in his

[33]

2

mind, it is so closely identified with his body and its biological struggle for survival that he loses his true alignment with the spiritual pole of his being. He forgets the heaven which is his intended home even on earth and he misconceives the creative principle within him, by virtue of which he is both unique and universal, as an ego belonging only to himself. He fancies himself, as no animal can or does, to be a separate, isolated unit in uneasy or hostile relationship with a world of similar units. And this illusion the prevailing conditions of earthly life, as well as the ancestral memories which he inherits, tend to strengthen as he grows from infancy to manhood.

Yet deep within him he knows, like the prince of many legends, brought up in a poor cottage, or the prodigal of Jesus's parable, that he has lost his birthright. And there comes a time in the history of every soul when he begins to ask who he really is and sets out in search of his father's kingdom.

In this eternal quest for a true identity Yoga and depth psychology offer guidance and help. Both, as I have said, assume that the individual has lost his true centre in becoming self-conscious. He is, therefore, falsely related to that infinite realm of consciousness and of life which envelops the little point of awareness to which his ego confines him. This infinite realm or sphere which contains man and which he contains in miniature within himself has, as I have suggested, its dark and its light hemispheres. Within the one we evolve in time as souls. Within the other we eternally know and are, as spirit. In the dark hemisphere of Nature the light of an indivisible Reality is hidden, but, like leaven in the lump, it works to inform the substance of life with meaning.

It is thus that consciousness evolves in the darkness or dimness of natural life. But there comes a time when the mental principle involved in the body of life emerges, as Sri Aurobindo puts it, "to meet and join with the supramental light and power descending from super-nature". This is the moment in the history of every soul when we first realize that we must be born again from above, that in our ascent from the unconscious depths, into which we plunged when we were born, we have reached a point when we must take responsibility for our future development, must recognize that the natural forces which have sustained and moulded our development so far, have now to be spiritualized by a conscious know-ledge which is to be won from a different plane of our being, from that plane in which the light shines by its own radiance and not by reflection, the plane of eternal truth.

At this moment we accept consciously the task of self-knowledge, of knowing, and so of becoming, what we truly are. This necessitates a knowledge of ourselves, not only as temporal beings subject, like all creatures of earth, to natural law and to the limited evolution which those laws allow, bound, too, to our primitive animal past, but also as spiritual beings in whom burns, however dimly, a light of pure intelligence which relates us to a realm of freedom and timeless value. The whole technique of Yoga and the condition of "union" at which it aims is based upon a recognition of this transcendent realm.

To what extent, we may ask, does depth psychology, implicitly, if not explicitly, recognize it too? Let us briefly examine the two approaches to the true centre which both seek, the one directing its gaze primarily to the super-terrestrial and super-sensuous spheres to which religion has always aspired, the other exploring the feminine depths of the psyche and winning from them a revealing and re-leasing mythology.

3

The union which the practice of Yoga is meant to induce is, with the spiritual principle, uniquely present in each

[35]

and all of us, of which our self-centred personality is an ignorant parody. This Atman, as it is called in Vedanta, is essentially what Christian mystics call the Christhood or Buddhists call "the Suchness". It is the indwelling Light which shines steadfastly and unattached within every form which life assumes, a consciousness which does not dissolve diversity but comprehends it in its own unity. In Yoga the individual is taught how he may become aware, in all he thinks and feels and does, of this spirit which is his real self and so resolve the conflict which is life-destroying whether we repress or express it.

For example Krishna declares in the *Bhagavad-Gita*: "He must fix his mind and heart upon the Atman and never think of anything else. No matter where the restless mind wanders, it must be drawn back and made to submit to the Atman alone."

It is often assumed that to fix the mind and heart upon the Atman involves repudiating the temporal realm in which we have our roots as physical and vital beings. But no practitioner of a true Yoga is asked to do this. By fixing his mind and heart upon the Atman, by recollecting moment by moment the spirit which inwardly informs him and all else, he ceases to identify himself with the transitory outer-movement of life in which his ego is immersed and enslaved. In this way he gradually discovers a centre of meaning in himself which relates him meaningfully to the world about him. By patiently freeing himself from mental distractions, by purifying his feelings and chastening the greed of his senses, he allows the light of truth to penetrate and pervade his whole being.

The true aim, in fact, of all religious exercises and disciplines is to allow the spiritual consciousness to recreate body and mind in the likeness of itself. Ordinarily we manifest very imperfectly the true light of our being. But by submitting ourselves mindfully to this light in all we think and feel and do, our very substance, so Yoga teaches, can be changed; the ancient depths of the unconscious can be gradually irradiated, until what is called "the glorious body" comes to birth.

It is quite wrong, then, to suppose that Yoga disregards the subhuman realm from which the evolving body and soul of man have emerged. These psycho-physical depths have, in fact, been profoundly explored in the East. The Tantric Yoga of northern India, for example, is based upon a unique knowledge of what Western psychology calls the "libido". But Yoga views this realm as subordinate to a higher one in which consciousness is supreme. And it is by identification with this plane of pure, uninvolved spirit that it seeks at once to deliver the self-centred individual from bondage to the realm of ancient instinct, and to re-establish him in true communion with it.

The analyst, who helps his patient to become conscious of the hidden forces which dominate his nature and of the shadowy forms which are unassimilated aspects of himself, has the same aim in view. A short passage from a book called *Journey into Self* by Esther Harding, an able disciple of Jung, will make clear what happens in a successful experiment in depth.

Jung has shown that when a human being explores the hidden depths of his own psyche he finds primordial images, pictures of racial experience, archetypes, ancient powerful forces which have influenced his character and actions all unseen and unknown. His personal ego no longer dominates the scene, his personal satisfactions fade into relative insignificance, and he becomes aware for the first time of the drama of inherited forces within himself. He realizes that the ego is no longer the centre of his psyche, the king of life. His consciousness enlarges and as the work of exploration proceeds and he strives for and attains a relationship to these figures, a new centre of consciousness gradually emerges.

[37]

This is not a new ego – a kind of super-I – for it includes racial and supra-personal trends which are not identical with the personal wishes and needs of the individual, though these also are represented. On the contrary, it has a non-personal quality which would prevent the individual from using the term "I" to express this new centre or self. In this new self may be found a supra-personal value which has for us moderns the power and validity which men in other times found through an ideal related to the external world or through the experience of a concretized religion.

This, then, is what a successful analysis in depth, as distinct from a mere untying of the tangles in the personal sub-conscious, can, it is claimed, achieve. Jung has called this new self "the total, timeless man", in whom the conscious and the unconscious are reconciled. Centred in it, the individual realizes that he is an immortal soul at one, not only with his racial past, but with the totality of being; and in this soul the psyche, which Jung has called "a contradictory plurality of complexes", is unified.

Only those who have enjoyed this psychological conversion can convincingly testify, by what they are, to its virtue. And the fact that so complete a transformation would seem to be exceptional – Jung himself describes it as "a relatively rare occurrence" – is no disproof of its essential value. Compared, however, with the methods of Yoga and of other traditional religious disciplines this journey into the depths of self does appear to dispense with a great deal which has hitherto been considered essential to the redemption of fallen human nature.

Like a novelist or dramatist in the toils of creation, the individual who submits to such analysis draws from his unconscious depths the substance of his own story, which is, also, a particular version of the arche-typal story of the human race. In doing this his creative imagination is called

into play both during sleep when he dreams and in inter-
preting the symbolism of his dreams when he wakes. If he
completes his story to his satisfaction, he experiences that
sense of unity, of creative necessity which every artist
knows in his happiest moments. But unlike the artist, who
is seldom permanently transformed by this experience,
however often he may repeat it, the subject of a successful
analysis, we are to suppose, becomes a new man, creatively
integrated and fulfilling his own particular nature, in
harmony with the universal spirit. This is what Jung calls
"individuation".

Clearly the particular value of the Jungian introspective
technique is that, by basing itself on the dreamer, it under-
cuts the stultifying self-consciousness by which so many
people today are pinioned. The individual who begins to
ponder the meaning of his dreams is imperceptibly drawn
away from his isolated selfhood and participates in the past
history of the human soul. Not only the instinctual, but the
moral and spiritual life of mankind throughout the ages,
lies hidden in the depths of the psyche. And the various
figures or archetypes which haunt the dreaming mind,
particularly such figures as the primordial Father and
Mother, or the "Wise Old Man", or the "Friend", are symbols of man's experience of a reality greater than himself.

Of this experience we are all heirs, who have failed to
take possession of our inheritance. In fact, as the analyst
shows, the inheritance can often take disastrous possession
of us. Depth-analysis can help people to realize in themselves something of the great impersonal drama in which
they play a part and to which they are called to relate
themselves creatively.

But can its exclusively subjective approach to these
mysteries, where they lie hidden in the feminine depths
of the unconscious, stored up in the memory of the great
anonymous Mother of us all, do more than make the
individual conscious that he is a living soul? This new

awareness of one's own depth of being is, indeed, the indispensable ground of all creative growth. For without a soul ready to receive the light, transcendent spirit cannot do its transforming work.

But even if the individual, through a successful analysis, has begun to realize the "total, timeless man" which in essence he is, to allow that essence to take possession of every level of his nature and transform it must surely require a long-continued practice of conscious recollection for which the psychologist at present makes little or no provision.

Without such devotional practice, whether of head or of heart, we cannot open ourselves to that plane of ideal intelligence and love, supernatural and superhuman, which the arche-typal images, dredged from the dark waters of the "collective unconscious", imperfectly and obscurely reflect. Jung may deny the reality of such a metaphysical plane. But few have advanced far in the spiritual life without acknowledging and entering into communion with it.

The fascination of the mythological world is great and it may easily become a closed circle, unless the light by which we read its meaning is constantly invoked and renewed and the goal envisaged be one of spiritual freedom within and beyond it.

It is here that Yoga and the traditional teaching step in. Given the integrated basis which the modern psychological technique can, ideally, ensure, Yoga teaches us by meditative and other practices how to quicken within the soul a new kind of mind and allow our whole being to be directed and informed by it. This intuitive or contemplative faculty, which we are to cultivate, is quite distinct from our ordinary brain-thinking. Its insight is of another order than logical acuteness. It is the faculty by which we can respond to the inspiration of the eternal Word, which speaks in the silence of the soul.

Our ordinary thought is a reflex of our terrestrial environment and is bounded by it. But the contemplative faculty, whether it is directed upon the world without or within us, is the organ of that uncreated Light, which is the essence of ourselves.

It is this faculty, with its direct seeing, which Yoga requires us to develop in ourselves, not in the night of dreams, but in a daylight of full awareness. To this awakened vision Nature herself is no longer a phenomenal world, a world only of sensations and of desirable or repellent objects, but a world of symbol and meaning, and by it we know that the cosmos itself is a revelation of what we ourselves are.

Creative minds have always seen Nature thus, as reflecting a celestial beauty. And by deeply contemplating the forms of such spiritual vision, in word or pigment, stone or sound, we can discover, quite as effectively as by any introspective technique, the great reality to which we belong and participate in its truth and mystery.

This reality consists not only of warring antagonisms, of the age-old conflict between the demonic and the divine. It reveals itself, too, in the serene image of the Buddha seated on the lotus or in an Italian Master's painting of the Virgin Mother and her child or in those beings of wisdom and love who can come before the mind in meditation and transmit to us the virtue of their presence.

These celestial forms that image the perfect pattern to which we aspire link us, not with a past which we need to outgrow, but with the eternal present of the spiritual world.

Yoga, then, is a method, at once simple in principle and elaborate in its possible application to every level of our being and every activity in which we engage, by which we cultivate the pure consciousness of the real man whom depth psychology can help to release within us, and at the same time cease to identify ourselves with that part of our mind which merely reflects a world of objects and which is

2*

discoloured by our desire or aversion for such objects. Yoga, therefore, like all the traditional teaching, is based upon a moral as well as a mental choice.

Modern psychology is understandably suspicious of moral teaching, since conventional morality only perpetuates the conflict implicit in the self-centred condition. Nevertheless something more, surely, than analysis, even in depth, is required fully to resolve this conflict. It has first to be consciously acknowledged and faced. And it is in the field of action in which we have to choose between conflicting impulses that we first become aware of two levels of our being.

On the lower level we are exposed to desires or obsessions which draw their force from the vast reservoir or dynamo of instinctual life. Man's perversion of instinct is the "original sin" of the human race. But he has not only exploited his animal nature, but struggled to civilize it. And it is in struggling with the primitive forces of our nature that we become increasingly conscious of a force of another kind, a force of light which is the counterpart of the force of life. This light, which we call divine because it is unearthly and undying, reproves our pursuit of partial satisfactions and reveals values which are only crudely implicit in the economy of the natural world.

All moral effort, every attempt to obey what "conscience", however imperfectly, commends, implies a recognition in us of the need to identify ourselves with a timeless truth which alone gives meaning to our life in time. The more fully conscious we are of these eternal values and the more imaginatively we assimilate them, the nearer we are to the goal of enlightenment which Yoga conceives to be our true destiny.

Morality, then, when truly conceived and practised is no negative repression, but an act of creative discrimination and part of that unceasing attentiveness to our inner spiritual principle, which informs every branch and aspect

[42]

of the craft of union. In practising such traditional virtues as faith, charity, humility, truthfulness and dispassion we learn, more simply and directly than in any other way, that, essentially, we do not belong to the material world and that we need not be at the mercy of the subconscious forces which rule the physical and vital levels of our nature.

To detach ourselves from these forces is the necessary pre-condition for accepting and transforming them. Psychologists, it seems to me, too easily assume that we cannot really experience those disorientated aspects of ourselves which Jung has called "the shadow" or "the animus" and "anima" except through the mediation of dreams and their subsequent analysis. This may be true of many today who, in M. Schuon's words, "are crossing the threshold of ordinary consciousness, but in a dreaming state". Such people may not yet be sufficiently conscious in their true being to look deeply into themselves from a detached, super-sensible standpoint. For them a technique which employs the dream to reveal what underlies their semi-conscious personality can free them from blind automatisms and so prepare them for the moment when they awaken to the reality of a spiritual faculty within them and a spiritual world about them, which exist in their own right, informing history, but independent of it, whether it be our own personal history or that part of the human race whose history we inherit.

But to those who are more spiritually awake the traditional method of disinterested self-examination, of humble and lucid watchfulness, can, I think, be just as effective in making us aware of those aspects of ourselves which we have overlooked or repressed and which will remain negative and disruptive elements in our being, until we have recognized that they, too, are necessary to our spiritual development and, through a right acceptance, can be changed from destructive to creative forces.

[43]

For consciousness and life are not opposed in principle, but only in the divided man, whose morality can be as destructive of life and value as his lack of it. Yet the law, which on every level maintains the order and structure of the universe, cannot be disregarded. For it embodies the principles by which creation is made effective.

Yoga teaches that to transgress this order, this *dharma*, inherent in the heart of man as in the universe at large, and by which, as he becomes individually conscious, he can distinguish between right and wrong action, is to disturb the balance of the cosmos and to invite chaos to come again. It is, also, by the ineluctable law of *Karma*, of cause and effect, to incur a debt against life which will have to be paid, and not only by the individual transgressor, before the balance can be restored.

The idea which modern psychology has encouraged that our sins are not our own, that they are determined by forces within and without us which we are powerless to resist is a half-truth which, if mistaken for the whole truth, reduces us to the status of children, whatever our age in years may be. Doubtless many of the patients whom the psychologist treats are still injured children or at best confused adolescents. And such people are certainly still too ignorant of themselves to tread the spiritual path of Yoga profitably. No one, in fact, who is uncritically subject to the compulsions of pride, passion, vanity, resentment, anger, envy or fear, can begin to tread it. Nor, for that matter, can such people come near the "deep centre" which is the goal of Jung's teaching, until these knots have been untied. It is obviously of little use to remind a severely maladjusted person that he is essentially a moral being.

Yoga, in fact, assumes that those who are prepared to tread the spiritual path which it discerns are sufficiently adult to accept responsibility for their thoughts, feelings and acts, however conditioned these may be by forces in the past or the present which are as yet difficult to control.

And if moral responsibility and discrimination is the indispensable basis of all true Yoga, it is, of course, only one factor in the restoration of our divided nature to unity and wholeness which the practice of this ancient spiritual science intends.

4

A true Yoga, then, affirms, quite as radically as "depth psychology", that man is the whole of his psyche, instinctual and spiritual, and that although in the early stages of his conscious development he is involved in unavoidable conflict and the pain which the struggle to resolve this conflict engenders, yet all this conflict and pain exist only to purify and educate his heart and mind. They are the world-illusion in which he has been ensnared, and when he awakes from it to a full awareness of that which he really is, the feud in him between beast and angel and all the other opposites is seen to have been unreal.

But for Yoga it is from the plane of transcendent spirit, of pure consciousness, that this victory over ignorance is won – a victory that is not a defeat of the natural powers and instincts, but an enlightening of them. Man begins to be self-conscious in close association with the lower realm of matter, of the "Not-I", through a body formed to live and enjoy natural life. Through instinct and feeling he has far more knowledge of this realm than of himself. But the pull of the spiritual pole of his being is always there, even when he is most deeply immersed in the primal waters. At that stage in his development the ideal order and intelligence of the spiritual world are imaged in the terrestrial archetypes which haunt his dreams and are enshrined in his myths, many of which symbolize man's age-old struggle to break from the stifling embrace of Mother Nature and be reborn in the freedom of the supernal Father's light.

But as that light grows in his mind, he begins to make direct contact, through the mediation of ideas and through powers of thought and will, with a timeless intelligence which alone gives meaning to our struggle to evolve and awaken in time. He awakens spiritually. The ideas of the good, the true and the beautiful, for example, and all the subtle modulations of this great trinity, shine like stars in the heaven of the mind and irradiate heart and will. These are the sacred norms of the spiritual world.

Today any conception of a realm of pure ideas is generally dismissed as a mere abstraction of unrooted minds in flight from existential truth. This is because contemporary man is generally so involved in material things and the physical and mental faculties required to handle them that he cannot conceive of ideas as transforming powers. Even psychology would seem to assume too readily that the idea must lack the vital and transforming virtue of the sublunary image. This is certainly true of the concepts of discursive thought which neither release hidden energy nor work any vital change in the person who handles them as logical or dialectical counters. That is why intellectual or abstract thinking man is, as Professor Price has admitted, something of a split personality and, as such, a little mad.

But the creative idea does not belong to the mental surface of our being. It does not derive from sensory experience or perceptible fact, but from a realm of timeless meaning. It is born invisibly of the union in our hearts of consciousness and life. As Maurice Nicoll wrote: "What illuminates us suddenly as *idea* is a perception of an order of life above us – an order of higher facts." The *idea* that we belong to this life and derive our reality from it and not from the world of the bodily senses opens for us a new dimension of experience.

In this a creative idea differs from many of the symbolic images which arise in dreams to protect us from truths too difficult or harsh to be understood in their nakedness. But when, in joy and humility, we are blessed by the birth of an idea, which is the substance of reality itself, and nourish it with love and care, the barrier between our waking and our dreaming mind is broken down. We enter what Ramana Maharshi has called "the state of waking sleep", of direct cognition. We are delivered from the logic of disquiet.

These are the kind of ideas which Yoga invokes and invites us to contemplate and make our own. The idea of the One in whom the two unite, for example, or that of "the Void" of Mahayana Buddhism, can be as potent objects of contemplation, of inner perception, as an actual image of Krishna or of the Buddha. In their purest form such ideas owe nothing to sensuous imagery, but exist only as pictures in the mind. They may be likened to rays emanating from an invisible sun, which contain within them the light of the supreme intelligence of which we and all creation are an expression. By deeply contemplating them and conforming our natures to the metaphysical truth which they contain we recover by degrees the true pattern of our being, the pattern of that pure original nature which, through ignorant self-will, we have lost. For we are, each of us, a creative idea in process of evolving its predestined form.

In the experience of the "deep centre" of Jungian psychology, the soul, rising like a lotus-bud from the muddied depths of the primordial waters, begins to open to the rays of this invisible sun. This is made possible to the extent that the mind, through analysis, has been freed from the complexes which entangled it, and the divided ego, through an assimilation of its unconscious components, has been displaced as the centre of the personality. In the new centre the multiple aspects of the psyche are unified. For this centre is the mysterious heart of life itself, in which spirit and substance meet and a cosmos creates itself moment by moment. But this experience, profound as it

[47]

doubtless can be in those in whom it is more than a passing intimation, is only a beginning.

Yoga is one of the traditional methods by which this first awakening to the inner life of the soul is consciously maintained and developed. For the new-born soul needs, like the lotus-bud, to unfold its petals and offer its golden heart to its celestial lover, the sun, until its uplifted chalice is filled with light. And for this we need, as Krishna declared to Arjuna, to watch over our soul and so allow the spirit to quicken and nourish the wisdom that is within her.

The various disciplines and craft of Yoga, as of all the traditional teachings, are means by which, through sustained attentiveness, the meeting of soul and spirit, of being and consciousness may be refined and deepened and at last be fully consummated in a perfect marriage.

Doubtless it was time, as Jung has remarked, for the soul to have her say, for the realm of feeling to reveal its riches of meaning in dream and myth. It was necessary that psychology should expose the unreality or partiality of mental concepts and mental acts, ungrounded in living experience. In this fidelity to feeling and its immediate datum Jungian psychology fulfils a real need and has done invaluable work.

But in the degree that it disregards what Buddhism has called "the diamond sphere of transcendent reality", which over-arches our ordinary mind as the "collective unconscious" underlies it, contemporary psychology, it seems to me, is unduly earth-bound. As human beings, rooted in earth, we live within psycho-physical bounds. But by virtue of our inmost reality we are eternally free within the apparently closed circuit of mortality and are capable of the pure creative act. "If the soul looks to what is behind," wrote Proclus of initiation into the Mysteries, "it sees the shadows and illusion only of what is. If it turns into its own essence and discovers its own relations, it sees itself only;

but, if it penetrates more deeply into the knowledge of itself, it discovers the spirit in itself and in all order of things. And, if it reaches into its inmost recess . . . it can see the race of gods and the unities of all things even with closed eyes." The traditional teaching differs from depth-psychology in affirming far more explicitly the reality of this undying and infinitely unifying spirit and the ways by which, ultimately, by patient devotion and recollectedness, we may conform our whole being to it. To humanize the natural man, by integrating his divided faculties, is only a step, though a most important one, in our spiritual evolution. But what Jung calls "individuation" does not complete the task of possible transformation.

This re-creative task, which begins in the labour of accepting and understanding the primitive forces that rule the hidden levels of our nature and so becoming a living soul, can only be fulfilled when we fully awake, in mind and heart, to the immortal principle within us and, by knowing it to be our true Self, complete our humanity in the divine. For as we advance in spiritual awareness, the meaning of the Sacred, the beauty of holiness and of the supernatural values which a sacred art or a saintly life embody become real to us as the ultimate measure of our human strivings. And it is by recognizing and reverencing this ideal, which psychology in its fidelity to the natural order distrusts, however far we may be from realizing it, that the union in us of the depth and the height is maintained.

In conclusion, then, one might venture to say, using the traditional terms of Christian mysticism, that a successful analysis in depth can lead its initiate through hell and purgatory towards the threshold of the heavenly kingdom. But that to go forward into the full radiance of the Light and ultimately into conscious union with its source, a more sacred science is required.

FRUITS OF SILENCE

Doubtless this is a goal to which few at present attain or even aspire. But he who treads the path of union faithfully has begun to learn that there is no goal to be attained. For what we really are has no beginning and no end. Our task in time is to realize *that* with every fibre of our being.

✿

CHAPTER THREE

Yoga and its Background

1

Western philosophy today is, at its best, a mental science, with all the precise analytical virtues of a science. But it is not philosophy in the ancient meaning of the word. For it confines itself to that which can be grasped by the logical mind, and so excludes all that such a mind cannot know. Yet the realm of the mentally unknowable, as the ancient philosophers well understood, is integral to wisdom – it is the mysterious realm of the heart, and true wisdom is born of a marriage of heart and head.

There have been sophistical schools in the long and insatiable history of Eastern speculation about life and its meaning. But they have never hitherto succeeded in cutting the roots of that tree which India's early sages planted so firmly, the tree which had primary roots in heaven or spirit, and secondary on earth or in nature, and which ensured for the evolving soul of man a fruitful intercourse between the realms of life and of light.

It was Descartes who founded in the West "the school of suspicion" with his dictum, *"de omnibus dubitandum est"*: we must doubt everything. But, before Descartes, Donne had declared that "New Philosophy calls all in doubt". Ancient philosophy in East and West was an expression of faith – of a faith tirelessly tested. It was not an exercise in negative analysis which is what modern scientism, masquerading as philosophy, generally is. The traditional philosophy, of which the thought of India is only the most ancient example on record, was an exercise in imaginative thinking. Such thinking, like every creative adventure of the human mind, maintains a fruitful tension between faith and reason. Nor is it limited, as most of our thought is today, to the world known to the physical senses and critically measured by that part of the mind which is tied to these senses.

The thinker of old was convinced by the exercise of his spiritual intelligence, a higher faculty than the physical mind, that he had access to a superconscious realm of truth as objectively real on its own inward plane as the landscape of the earth. He trained himself to see into this realm by developing his intuitive vision. That was why he was called a seer. It was with the forms and patterns of meaning revealed to him in this inner realm that he was concerned, and not with the mechanisms of physical life which engross almost entirely the interest of contemporary Western man.

How the natural world works can, in time, be grasped and mastered by a shrewd onlooker with the aid of measuring rods and instruments. It is otherwise with its meaning and the spiritual intelligence required to see it. Here the whole person is involved. "What is the price of Experience?" asked William Blake,

> do men buy it for a song?
> Or wisdom for a dance in the street? No, it is
> bought with the price
> Of all that a man hath. . . .

To discover the meaning of life on any level of its manifestation we need to participate in a mystery of which we and all things are a part, with all our faculties cleansed and dedicated to the task.

The thought of India, from the earliest times, was directed towards such an act of participation. To this end its sages lived the meaning which they expounded, and taught their pupils as much by what they were as by their words. They would have regarded intellectual analysis pursuing its researches in a sort of moral vacuum as only a refinement of ignorance. And it was from this ignorance in all its forms that they invited their disciples to awake.

This ignorance is not just a mental ignorance. It is the universal darkness in which we and the world, as we dimly see it, live, until the clear light of a true consciousness breaks through. In our struggle to emerge from the darkness we become self-conscious and acquire an ego through which we receive fitful gleams of the light we are seeking. But these we distort by appropriating them for our own ends. And so, despite all the painful and cruel errors which we commit, we remain blind to what we really are and mistake our spectre, as Blake called it, for the true principle of our being.

To become aware of this ignorance and to recognize that what we have been clinging to is an illusion, or at best a perversion of the real, is the basic aim of all the Eastern teachings, whether Hindu, Buddhist or Taoist. This recognition of the relative unreality of what is fleeting and phenomenal in ourselves and in the world we misread is, in the thought of India, the necessary condition of discovering the reality which informs and transcends it.

This Reality they named Brahman, in its cosmic aspect, and Atman as the universal "I" which underlies the mutable mask which each of us dons in the process of adjusting ourselves to a world apparently external to our senses. Brahman, the divine being and power that manifests as the world, and Atman, the divine principle within the human heart, are one. In each of us, as in every form of manifested life, this universal principle of being and consciousness finds unique expression, though in the lower forms of life its uniqueness tends to be submerged in the type. But in all its multiple expressiveness it is undividedly One.

A longing to recover this unity, within and beyond all difference, to share in the total drama of creation or, as primitive man imagined himself as doing, to re-enact "what the Gods did in the beginning", has underlain the religious experience of mankind throughout the ages. It has driven men equally to excesses of self-abandonment or extremes of asceticism according as they sought the abyss of the unconscious or the heights of enlightenment. In either case the impulse arose out of the fact that man, so far as he is subject to time, is a transient being. As such he is conditioned by his environment. Yet something in him is not so conditioned and the knowledge of this, however dim it be, moves him eventually to resent his bondage.

The need, in some way, to cease to be subject to the mutable forces of the temporal world is no less acknowledged in the Christian rite of baptism, in which "the world, the flesh and the devil" are abjured, than in the Yoga-sutras of Patanjali. Nevertheless Western man has today so successfully or disastrously come to terms with his temporal setting that he often seems content to regard himself as merely an historical episode or even an historical accident.

Indian thought, by contrast, has throughout the centuries remained faithful to the vision of its ancient sages and has devoted itself with zeal and subtlety to the study of man's conditionings and to developing a technique by which he may transcend them and so discover the jewel of spiritual freedom which lies hidden in his heart.

Yoga is the name given to this quest. The word has been so vulgarized in the West that one almost hesitates to use it. It means, of course, union, and the whole of Indian religion and culture is an expression, in one form or another, of the ideal and practice of union. Union with what? With That which we truly are, however we may conceive It and wherever It is to be found. Only in and by

[54]

such union, say the Indian sages, can we experience liberation or "Moksha", which is the goal of Yoga and the one sure proof of having attained it.

The liberated man or woman has rent the veil of "Maya", a word often misinterpreted in the West, and the meaning of which is not easily conveyed. Briefly one may define it as the divine "art" of creation by which spirit assumes form. But for the man who clings to the form for its own sake, it becomes the magic spell under which he lives, before he is enlightened. As such it creates the illusory world known to the grasping senses, the world in which man is immeshed, outwardly by all the visible and tangible things around him, and inwardly by the hungers and delusive satisfactions of his omnivorous self.

This world to which we are bound by so many ties of pleasure and pain and which exercises over us so continual a fascination that we can hardly conceive the possibility of another is, the Eastern sages say, a self-centred dream, without real substance, a mirage in a desert of desire. Only when we have learnt to see through it and found the reality which it so beautifully or terribly veils, can we know what freedom is or communicate it to others. Only then will physical experience cease to bind and blind us.

As Shankara wrote, "this whole multiplicity of creatures, existing under name and form, in so far as it has the Supreme Being itself for its essence is true; if regarded as self-dependent, it is untrue, or Maya."

Now it hardly needs saying that the path which leads to emancipation from the thraldom of Maya is as beset with false turnings as the one along which we plunge more and more deeply into Maya's illusive embrace.

Each one of us is closely attached by habitual impulses to an unregenerate life, a life determined by our unconscious assumption that we are, not unique beings, but separate entities. In this world of profane dualism subject

[55]

confronts object across a gulf, and however near the one may come to the other, the gulf imperceptibly remains. It is this dualism which Indian philosophy sets out to disprove by its non-dual teaching.

What, then, did the ancient *rishis* mean by the non-dual way? And what was the Oneness in which they declared the conflict of the opposites could be resolved? All their thinking is directed to unveiling a new kind of consciousness, which is hidden beneath the physical and psychic forces which constitute the world of change and which hold us captive to their vital spell. This consciousness is the imperishable Atman, the transcendental Self, uncreated but present in all created things and the blissful ground of their being.

To realize this Spiritual Presence a man must disentangle himself from the world that his selfish desires have spun around him, the world that he sees only or mainly in its phenomenal aspects. If he succeeds in this, he will still, in body and mind, be a creature of time and change, but he will no longer be attached to what is transient or, as a result of such attachment, in conflict with himself. For he will be centred in that which is eternal and undivided and which harmonizes in itself all the contraries of existence.

Living under the direction of his metaphysical principle or, in simpler words, "by the spirit", which animates every form of life, however humble or exalted, he will be in communion with all that is. The gulf which divides the self-centred individual, both inwardly and outwardly, will have closed. The way of wholeness of being and understanding will be open.

Now obviously no amount of argument will convince a man, who has not at least begun to experience directly in his own living this kind of spiritual consciousness, that such a radical transformation of himself is not only possible, but grounded in the nature of things and in the evolutionary purpose of life. It was for this reason that Indian philosophy, while acknowledging that the real agent of enlightenment is within ourselves, has so much emphasized the importance of a teacher who, by embodying the higher knowledge, can transmit it directly, as a lit candle can kindle the wick of another, as well as teaching the skill required for attaining and exercising it.

Yet even when a true teaching has been traditionally established, the risk of misconceiving it is very great, as the history of Indian thought and practice, and for that matter of all religious practice, all too sadly proves.

The basic temptation is always the same. It is to conceive of timeless spirit as opposed to the life of time, from which, therefore, man's only hope is to escape. In fact the basic aim of all true Yoga was and is liberation *in* life. But this involves doing the opposite of what unregenerate life demands that we should do. At first sight, therefore, Yoga can seem to involve the rejection of life. And this has hitherto been the common view of it in the West. But it is a false view. It is not to divide Time and Eternity that the Yogi undertakes his arduous task of re-creation, but to restore to them their true relation in the human heart and mind.

The world-and-life-denying impulse, so generally associated in the West with the Eastern teachings, is not of their original essence. It is rather a perversion which has crept into them again and again in the course of their development and has its roots, according to Heinrich Zimmer * in a remote non-Vedic, Indian antiquity.

This earth-repudiating view was in sharp conflict with the buoyant affirmation of the unity of all life which the Aryan poet-seers hymned in the *Vedas* and expounded with such subtle insight in the *Upanishads*. One of the earliest and shortest of these, the *Isha Upanishad*, provides

* In *Philosophies of India* by Heinrich Zimmer.

the classic statement of this integral vision. Its central idea is the creative relation of apparent opposites and primarily of the One and the many, which meet in Brahman, who contains all and also inhabits all.

In this ancient Aryan faith there is no real conflict between the multiple movement of the manifesting universe and the unborn and unchanging genius of which it is an expression. Man, therefore, has only to identify himself with the genius of his being to participate, free from pain and illusion, in all the divine play of life and death through which Brahman reveals his truth and splendour. For, in the words of the *Upanishad*:

he who sees everywhere the Self in all existence and all existences in the Self, shrinks not thereafter from aught.

In other words he has discovered within himself the non-duality, the experience of not being two, in which the "I" and the "not-I" enter into true relationship.

But this Vedantic non-duality in which the faith of the Aryan invaders culminated was alien to the primordial belief of the dark-skinned Dravidian people. The latest archaeological research suggests a close religious kinship between the aboriginal inhabitants of India and the contemporary peoples of the Middle East, who worshipped the Earth Mother as a symbol of the unity of all life. This worship, fusing later with the Aryan faith, emerged in the rites and mysteries of the Tantra, with its cult of Shakti, the goddess spouse of Shiva, and of the female principle as the projected energy of the male.

The Tantra embodied, to some extent at least, a synthesis of Aryan idealism and Dravidian realism. The Aryans aspired to the eternal and the super-conscious, the Dravidians were rooted in time and the sub-conscious. The emphasis in the one was solar and patriarchal, in the other matriarchal and lunar. The truest wisdom and the greatest

[58]

art of Hinduism has sprung from the creative embrace of these two traditions, the one aspiring heavenward, the other obedient to its earthly origin. But the polarity has always been precarious, as it is in every developing human consciousness, which is apt to alternate between one or other extreme, as life's pendulum swings. And the underlying theme of the great epics of India, the *Ramayana* and the *Mahabharata*, is the struggle between the forces of darkness and light, between a black and a white magic, which has to be fought out before a true balance between the two poles can be established. An earth-repudiating view may be associated with an ecstatic contemplation of the uncreated Brahman. But it may equally emerge from the worship of the Earth Mother. For, as both mythology and psychology show, man at a certain stage of development, has to struggle hard to disentangle himself from the dark embrace of physical life, to find freedom as an individual and to become spiritually conscious. In his struggle he may well be tempted to deny his earthly conditions or view them as inherently evil.

Some such morbid repudiation, it would seem, had to some degree infected the dualistic outlook of the Dravidians or later developed through the inter-action of their way of thought and spiritual experience and that of the Aryan invaders. Particularly in the north-east of India, where the influence of the Aryans was least strong, the idea of a permanent enmity between heaven and earth, the realms of spirit and of matter, increasingly possessed men's minds. In this deeply pessimistic view of things to repudiate physical life was a virtue. The one aim to be pursued by every kind of heroic austerity and mortifying exercise was escape from the physical bondage in which man found himself.

But the victory which was to crown these grim endeavours was not of life purified and made new or of a humanity regenerated, individually and socially – it was a sterile

victory over life, an out-and-out rejection of the human
condition, and a total triumph of the immaculate and
implacable spirit over the tainted body in which some
obscure fate had imprisoned it in a dismal round of birth,
death, and re-birth.

Such a negative view of earthly life, when it fused with
the Aryan faith, was much modified. In Jainism this fusion
seems to have occurred least and it is in Jainism that its
extreme tenets and practices survive most clearly. But its
influence can be seen and felt in the Samkhya philosophy
of Kapila and the Yoga sutras of Patanjali and also in the
teachings of Gautama, the Buddha, at least in the form in
which they have come down to us.

Again in the eighth century A.D. we can detect its presence
under the disguise of a professed non-dualism in the more
extreme statements of the saintly poet and subtle logician,
Shankara, who set out to restore the pure Vedantic teaching in a degenerate age, but who, in his commentaries,
repeatedly stressed the incompatibility between knowledge as the spiritual goal and action in the world.

Opinion is divided as to whether Shankara's own interpretation of the Advaita teaching reduced the material
world in which we have to live and act to a mere illusion
or not. But there can be no doubt that his commentaries,
and particularly that on the *Bhagavad-Gita*, were am-
biguous enough to encourage such an illusionist and
escapist view – a view to which the *Gita* itself is fundamentally opposed. And unfortunately it is this interpretation of the ancient scriptures, which has been accepted
until recently in the West as the first and last word of
Eastern wisdom.

Nevertheless without the challenge of this Dravidian dualism, which had its positive as well as its negative side, the
Aryan faith might have remained no more than an idealistic
affirmation. The positive aspect of the indigenous culture
was emphasized by Rabindranath Tagore when he wrote:

The old Dravidian culture should in no way be under-rated: the result of its combination with the Aryan was the Hindu civilization, which acquired both rich-ness and depth from the Dravidians. They may not have been introspective or metaphysical, but they were artists, and they could sing, design and build. The transcenden-tal mind of the Aryan by its marriage with the emotional and creative art of the Dravidian gave birth to an off-spring which was neither fully Aryan nor Dravidian, but Hindu.

And in religion and philosophy the realism of the old indigenous belief compelled the visionaries to put their faith to the test of the actual world, with all its pains and miseries and the feverish havoc wrought by man's self-centred desires. The vision of the Oneness of the Cosmos and of man could only be truly vindicated when it had taken up into itself and redeemed all that so cruelly seemed to deny it. The teaching and the practice of Yoga acknowledged this necessity, and were devoted to this task.

2

What, then, was and is the goal which Yoga sets before man as the one essential quest for a human being, endowed with the potentialities of consciousness? It is the realiza-tion of the divine principle within him, of that Sole Being and pure consciousness, unseen and ungraspable, which, in his own way, he shares with every form of life and by virtue of which he can transcend his divided status and enjoy communion with All that lives.

His task, then, is to remove, in whatever way proves most suitable to his nature and to his degree of spiritual development, all that hinders this realization and keeps him enclosed in a cocoon of ignorance, not only of his own true nature, but of the real world in which he moves. Man draws ever nearer to this realization through the disillusioning process, slow but eventually sure, of earthly living. But though this may prepare him for the moment of awakening, something more intensive is required to bring it about. Yoga, in its various forms, is that something. It is the catalyst which precipitates the organic redisposition of the individual's faculties round a new centre.

Now such a task, if it is self-consciously undertaken, exposes a person to one especial temptation – that of repudiating life; in fact to the very dualism which it is the purpose of a true Yoga to resolve. For perhaps the greatest hindrance to the desired awakening is the bondage which the senses exercise over us. It is through our senses that from earliest infancy we experience life on a physical level and though, as our intelligence grows, we recognize how fallible these senses can be and that there are realms of experience which are, to a large extent, independent of them, most of us have by that time become their habitual captives through the desires which we have gratified through them. Consequently we persistently identify ourselves not with our spiritual being, of which we have as yet a scanty knowledge, but with our earth-bound and earth-conditioned nature.

The fault, however, is in ourselves and not in the supposedly evil nature of matter or the inherent viciousness of bodily appetite. The evil is not in them, but in our corrupting attachment to them, which prevents us from growing spiritually and so learning to experience life unpossessively, not only through the physical senses, but through those higher faculties, intuitive, aesthetic, and, in the purest sense of the word, moral, by virtue of which we are distinctively human and ultimately more than human. We need, therefore, to rid ourselves of this attachment without turning against life on any of its levels.

In every perverse form of Yoga, whether Eastern or

Western, life is rejected in some degree. But while we must condemn such rejections, we need to remember how powerful the attachment is from which release is sought – so compulsive, indeed, that most people suppose that life could not function without it. It may well, therefore, be essential in the early stages of learning the art of non-attachment to withdraw for a time, so far as we can, from the cruder pressures and distractions of the world to obtain and establish a footing, through contemplation and other practices, in the inner world in which the spirit can be directly known. Such withdrawal need not imply a repudiation of life on any level on which it manifests, but only an inward change in our relation to it.

There are three main methods in classical Indian Yoga, by which the illusions of self-centredness may be outgrown and the peace and bliss of a being centred in the Atman may be attained. These may be distinguished as the Yogas of action, of devotion, and of contemplation, or, more simply, of work, of love, and of knowledge. They are not, of course, mutually exclusive. In different degrees each involves the others, and ultimately they coalesce.

Karma Yoga or the Yoga of action is directed to re-educating us on the everyday level of what we do, in whatever calling we may pursue, and in those countless acts we perform from morning to night, each one of them in some degree biased by self-will and to that extent uncreative. They are biased in the measure that we desire, consciously or unconsciously, some reward for ourselves, some private satisfaction in the doing of them. This desire deflects our attention from the act itself and the right performance of it to the end or the fruits of it. We are not wholly attentive to the task in hand, its medium, and the best means to accomplish it. At the worst the act is only regarded as a means to personal gain. It is of no importance in itself.

Through the discipline of Karma Yoga we cultivate acts

[63]

which are void of selfish will and its anxious desire for fruits. Gradually in this way, by a change of inner attitude, our acts cease to be self-enhancing and so find their true resting-place in the passive depths of our nature, those depths in which we are at one with the true rhythm of life itself. Such acts are only possible when all our intelligence and energy, our skill and sensitiveness are concentrated in the act itself and the laws which govern it, and in our relationship with the person or object involved in the act. This actionless action cannot, in fact, be achieved in a merely neutral or indifferent state of mind. It would not be a truly disinterested act, if it were not also a devoted and dedicated act, as every real craftsman knows. And it fulfils itself in self-forgetful service of one's neighbour.

Karma Yoga is thus inevitably related to Bhakti Yoga, the Yoga of devotion. The aim of this Yoga is to purify feeling as Karma Yoga purifies the will. Feeling is notoriously possessive and even when it pours itself out in love of some person whom it cherishes, it is seldom undemanding. Bhakti Yoga recognizes this and it imposes no abrupt veto upon the impulsive or clinging tenderness of the heart's affections. But its purpose is to take the vital force which enraptures and tortures us through our feelings and to guide it into ever purer channels of worship and adoration. It shows us, little by little, that the absolute self-surrender, for which we blindly hunger in all our partial acts of love, can only come about when we have discovered in our own hearts the Presence and quintessence of love itself.

But this cannot be at once. The religion of love is for long inevitably dualist. To the devotee of Bhakti Yoga the Beloved is ultimately Ishvara, the supreme Lord who creates and sustains the Universe. He is worshipped as a Person both in himself and in and through forms which image his beauty, his truth and his powers, whether they be the forms of nature or of myth and ritual, or of an

[64]

inspired teacher who radiates the Light of the eternal. These concrete aids, which at once separate the lover from his Beloved and act as conductors of his grace and inspiration, are necessary in all but the final stages of the devotional path.

But by constant recollection of the Beloved, who may be imaged in the feminine as well as the masculine mode, and by constant renunciation of the self in the act of loving him, for no other reward than the bliss of knowing how lovable he is, the devotee is drawn into ever closer union with the object of his love. For the divine lover whom he seeks, though he seems to attract him from without, also and more essentially directs him from within. There, indeed, he is to be found when the heart has become pure enough to hold him. Then the veils of separation dissolve and love, lover and Beloved are one.

The way of Bhakti Yoga is thus the easiest and most natural way to liberation and for that very reason, in its early stages, the hardest, through the power of attraction which life exerts over our lower nature through our feelings. We cannot counter or transmute this attraction by our own efforts. It is the Supreme Love at the heart of things, embraced in faith, gratitude, reverence and adoration, which enables us to outgrow the wants that bind and blind us.

Through what we suffer in our partial and passionate attachments the dross in our natures is consumed in the flame of love's relentless truth, provided our devotion to that greater love and our willingness to bear its burning rays are constant. The nearer we come to living that love, the less do we grasp at some object which excites and attracts our feeling. For we both feel and know the presence in our own hearts, as in all else, of a perfect love which comprehends us and draws us into a communion of life and understanding with all that is. By such love we are wholly delivered from the self.

Thus love, in dying to self, grows lucid. For deep devotion, by relaxing all mental tension, leads us to the heart of real Being. And in that heart shines the light of perfect awareness. But this enlightenment may be sought from the mental rather than the emotional side of the nature. And this is the approach of Jnana Yoga or the Yoga of knowledge, of which the method is that of concentration, meditation and contemplation in their many forms. This is far too vast a field to begin to explore here. But it may help to define in a word or two the common aim of all such inward practices.

This is to still the external activities and preoccupations of that part of our mind which we have developed as an instrument of our self-centred plans and purposes, whether theoretical or practical, by observing them from within and separating ourselves from them. Thus it gradually becomes possible to experience and express another kind of intelligence, the creative consciousness which is the organ of our higher mind.

Those who have seriously practised meditation will not need convincing that such a consciousness is a reality and that it differs, not merely in degree, but in kind from our ordinary everyday mentality. Both qualitatively and in its genius for comprehending and harmonizing our sensory experience and the conflicting thoughts by which we are constantly assailed, it proves itself to be at once the central light of our being and the universal mind which oversees and underlies the cosmos of which we are meant to be the human centre.

It is through a gradual or sudden transference of our physical, mental and moral faculties from the control of self-consciousness to that of spiritual awareness that we find this true centre and learn to think and feel and act from it.

Until this transference has taken place, self-control, however necessary, involves a division in us between the will which controls and the impulses which are controlled. The resulting tension constricts our response to life and can become in time quite paralysing, even splitting the psyche in two, as in the victims of schizophrenia. From this tight-jacket which grips us the more firmly, the more self-consciously we try to wriggle out of it, the Yoga of Knowledge can release us by enlightening our understanding. It gives us a new idea of what we are, and this revolutionizes our way of living, if we practise it. For a real idea is a living force once it is truly taken in and assimilated. By making us conscious of our inner potentiality, where before we were ignorantly struggling for outer survival, this Yoga releases us from the paralysis of self-will into that centre of being in which we are at once inspired and controlled by a greater will than our own.

The Yoga of knowledge includes all the meditative practices, so various in both method and content to suit the needs of different people, which can enable us to achieve this radical change from a divided mentality to a unified and intuitive awareness, of which love is the flower.

3

Such a brief and cursory account of the three principal schools of Yoga, of which there are a number of specialized sub-divisions, will at least show that they all have the same end in view. In the *Bhagavad-Gita* Krishna brings them together, as he concludes his teaching, relating them to Himself as an incarnation of the divine.

"Place your mind in Me," he says, or, in other words, "devote your thinking to the task of knowing Me." "Be My devotee," that is, "centre your heart in love and worship of Me." And finally or it may be, firstly, "Serve Me," or "consecrate all your actions by offering them to Me." In the Indian view, however, valuable as a personal image of the divine can be to many as a focus for contemplation, particularly on the devotional path, it is not essential. The Yoga of Patanjali's sutras, based on the Samkhya philosophy, is, for example, devoid of any presumption of a personal God. So too, is the Yoga of Buddhism.

Yet the aim, in all its branches, is the same – to deliver those who practise it from the distractions and illusions of the unreal self and to integrate them in reality itself.

To many Westerners, however, this aim which is common to all traditional Indian spirituality, seems to involve a denial or at least an evasion of the necessary, if tragic struggle in which man is called to play his part on earth.

So far, indeed, as the Western view has stressed the actuality of man's divided state and the need for him resolutely to confront his shadow-self as a condition of any possible redemption, it has been a true view. That the bright and dark angels, the dove and the serpent, are true symbols of our dual human personality, experience daily proves. Nor can there be any creative growth except through the meeting of these contraries. But a contemporary Western psychologist would, I think, agree with an enlightened Eastern teacher that the conflict between them is a phase which we are meant to outgrow.

Just as a plant must root itself in the dark soil before it can rise into the clear air and unfold in aspiration to the sun, so the spirit or pure consciousness which lives in man had to take root in its apparent opposite and be condensed in the dark unconsciousness of matter that so it might assume a form and, through many stages of growth, evolve ultimately an expressive image of itself.

The world of conflict which the West has made its own, and in which it has achieved the glories of Chartres and the infamies of Buchenwald, is one of these stages, that in which man becomes self-conscious, enters the realm of divided experience and learns in it to make distinctions and difficult decisions and play a part, heroic or craven or most often neither one nor the other, in the human drama through which the eternal unfolds its meaning in time.

With this stage history in the West has made us so familiar that we have come to regard it as the term of human possibilities and any religion or philosophy which affirms the power of spirit to evolve further is viewed with the gravest suspicion.

But the Eastern Masters, as, indeed, Jesus of Nazareth, have always assumed that man's task on earth is not only to acquire self-knowledge and self-control in the conflict between his vital and moral impulses, but ultimately to resolve this conflict at a higher and deeper level in himself.

What they ask of their disciples is not a cowardly disengagement from the ordeal of human life and our shared responsibilities, but a profounder engagement, a fearless commitment to the necessity of outgrowing the diseased condition of self-conscious man and becoming whole in heart and mind and will.

They teach that there awaits all of us, who have faithfully endured the burden and heat of the day of bound "experience", a further stage – that of enlightenment and freedom. It is with this stage that they are primarily concerned and which they have explored and elucidated with such subtle insight.

Since most of us are normally engaged during our early life in the struggle to define and distinguish ourselves amid the stresses and testings of the market-place and the home, the teaching and practice of Yoga are more apt to the needs and opportunities of the second half of life than the first. But in reality a non-dualist view of things alters the perspective in which we see the whole of man's adventure on earth and the kind of life which, from childhood onwards, we would do well to cultivate.

That there are dangers and perversities in the non-dual

way as taught in some schools of Yoga, no impartial student of the Eastern teachings would deny. But the perils of continued bondage to the profane dualism in which Western man has come to acquiesce are now clearly so great that he can ill afford to turn a deaf ear to the ancient wisdom.

❀

CHAPTER FOUR

Stepping Westward

1

There is a German fairy story which has comforted me when I have been tempted to think that the wounds which tragic circumstance inflict on the very young can never heal. In it a girl is asked to choose between a happy youth and a happy old age and decides for a happy old age so that she shall at least have something better to look forward to.

Life does not usually present such simple alternatives and, outside fairy stories, the present is the only time of which we can be sure and which, joyously or sorrowfully, we can make our own. We seldom do so because our minds are set on the future, if we are young, and turn back on the past when we are old. But the idyllic futures we dream of are generally those which can never exist. The past to which we return is a dream too, though it may be a sad one.

But the girl in the fairy story had at least enough faith in life to believe that it always had something to give and that it could even keep its best gifts to the last. When a civilization is dying, as is our own, or is threatened with disaster for want of the wisdom which the old should infuse into it, the young are understandably sceptical of such a belief. Maturity, if they are to judge it by the reasoned disillusionment or the dull conformity of most of their elders, is less the crown of life than its withering. The pace, too, at which life is lived today and the general engrossment in its physical and material aspects encourage the view that age, with its slower rhythm, is synonymous with disability, and this despite the fact that people in many parts of the world live active lives longer than they did. But such longevity is valued less as an opportunity for new and more sensitive experiments in living than for prolonging the kind of life which habit has stereotyped.

If to grow old is to learn to be as active in contemplation as once we were active in doing, it can be as rewarding an experience as growing up. For to grow in knowledge of the inner world is no less satisfying than to extend our grasp over the outer. Indeed its rewards are incomparably greater. Nor does contemplation deny the world of action and sensation. But it transforms our relation to that world and our vision of it. Above all it teaches us that we are born into life that we may learn to die into it. As long as we breathe, birth and death are never divided, strive as we do to force them apart. Spiritual death is, in different degrees, the measure of our success in separating them.

When life is at its physical spring, we are least inclined to do this. Youth with its gaiety and engaging abandon, if not borne on wings, carries on its back a quiver full of arrows, each a glinting possibility. Even the unfavoured of fortune have then a reserve of hope to draw upon and though this hope may attach itself to some object in view, some enterprise of the moment, or some goal ahead, it is in essence the aura or effulgence of life's belief in itself. In Gabriel Marcel's words, it is the "fuel that keeps a life alight from day to day".

"I remember my youth," wrote Conrad, "and the feeling that will never come back any more – the feeling that I could last forever, outlast the sea, the earth, and all men; the deceitful feeling that lures us on to joys, to perils, to love, to vain effort – to death."

When we are intoxicated by life on whatever level, we

are easily deceived, not by life, but by ourselves. For the sense that we have in youth of being infinitely alive is a true instinct, though its truth can only be proved by learning to live more and more consciously in That which never dies.

True hope is an inward assurance that life is endlessly creative, strong enough to outweigh its apparent defeats and failures. As we cease to be young, such hope has increasingly to stand the test of reflection. This it will fail to do unless we think so deeply into life that we reach to the very roots from which hope itself springs. To do this we may well need to despair of life and thus learn no longer to cling to it. But if, for any reason, we turn our minds against life in reflecting upon it, whether we disguise this hostility as critical analysis or common-sense realism, we shall lose hope and at best have to fall back on some philosophy of endurance or defiance, or on a hedonism by which we try to console ourselves through pleasure for our loss of joy.

Beneath all such stratagems is a sense of having been cheated by life and so of the need to outwit an untrustworthy opponent. And this distrust reflects a recoil of thought from the embrace of life, when the transition from unconscious to conscious intimacy is necessary, if we are to enter freely into its heart. It is, basically, a failure in love. But to say this is not very helpful until we have really learnt what it means and what it costs to love. Love is always an absolute venture of faith, a total acceptance of every relative loss, including, it may be, the apparent loss of love itself, and, above all, of the assertive self which we so habitually assume ourselves to be.

This is a lot to ask of the mind when it first begins to reflect upon life and sees it bristling with hazards and riven with conflicts. The need to survive, to compete, to conquer, so easily overrides the need to love. And life itself seems to approve and exemplify this. For there is no

[73]

human impulse which cannot find its apparent justification in the life of which we are a part and which mirrors what we are at any moment. The less partial we are in ourselves, the more meaning will life disclose to us and the more convinced we shall be of the need to accept life, not only at the high pitch of ecstatic experience, but even when all zest for living seems to fail. Only so shall we grow deeper and deeper into the nature of being.

It is because so many people are deaf to the living pulse of growth, hearing only the mechanical drone of the wheels of change, that they feel betrayed by life, when the infidelity is in fact their own. This is particularly true, perhaps, of fortune's favourites whom difficulty or deprivation have not taught to be patient and persist, or, at the other extreme, of the sensitive waifs whom fate has handled too roughly or tested too soon. The fact that age is so generally viewed only in its negative aspect as a disability, a contraction, a lengthening shadow cast by a sinking sun and drawing out to an end long anticipated with fear or resignation, shows how little the bounty of life is realized by those who have ceased to trust it.

Gustave Holst, in his interpretation of the Planets, named Saturn the planet of old age. As we listen to the music in which he expressed what Saturn meant to him, darkness or at least a sort of deadness or numbness envelops us. Bound like sacrificial victims to the anvil of existence, we can only wait for the pitiless hammer of the years to intensify its striking power and deal us the final blow.

Saturn, so conceived, does, indeed, symbolize one aspect of old age, to which we can hardly fail to give due weight – the fatality, as it seems, of being tied to a body that is always reminding us, with the rose of Edmund Waller's lyric, "how small a part of time we share" with the beauty that blooms and fades in a day. But Saturn, as symbolical mid-wife of existence, imposing limits on the limitless, is as much the planet of infancy as of old age. To be born is to plunge into mortality and so to die. Yet few weep or wring their hands over an infant's cradle. "I am but two days old" sings the infant of William Blake's lyric, and a thousand infants crying in the night do not contradict the truth that "joy is my name", a joy that declares life to be infinitely blissful in its essence, a joy whose victorious spirit can transform even a prison into a paradise.

It was the enraptured taste of this joy, when he was young, that made Wordsworth confident, even when time had chastened his instinctive response to it, that

> *Nature never did betray*
> *The heart that loved her; 'tis her privilege*
> *Through all the years of this our life, to lead*
> *From joy to joy.*

Yet Wordsworth, it may be said, failed, at least partially, to live out the faith which he so confidently affirmed, succumbing in middle life to that cramp of self-consciousness which is peculiarly the disease of the modern mind.

Nature, as mother of our instinctive life, knows nothing of this cramp, being spontaneously obedient to the spirit which informs her. But the same spirit works in man to wake him from the blissful sleep of instinct to look his Mother in the face. And the face he sees when he wakes is no longer that of the Mother who smiles comfortingly on all his needs, but of the Sphinx who gazes through him into some vast beyond, impassively contemplating his puny and often perverse efforts to break from her arms and shape his own destiny.

Yet how can he break free when hers is the body in which he draws his breath from the cradle to the grave? However far his intelligence may carry him, however subtly he may analyse the elements of that body, which is also his own, any freedom which he may claim in defiance of the spirit which she so perfectly obeys, will prove a worse bondage than the blind instinct which he would outgrow.

It is thus that Nature serves the growing soul in man, not only as a cherisher of life and joy, but also as a *mater dolorosa*, swaddling us in the sorrows of lack and loss, punishing us dispassionately for our transgressions of her law, and teaching us at each stage of the incarnation, which we have received from her, the lesson which we most need to learn. The less we are ready to learn, the harder do we find it to love her. Yet the love that informs her sternest judgement no less than her radiantly rewarding smile has only one end in view, to temper our hearts and minds to affirm the joy which is the essence of her being and which is beyond both loss and gain, as we self-centredly measure them. Without this ageless joy, equally present in old and young and only waiting to be purely known, the heart of life would cease to beat. But when it shines in eyes however old, eyes that tears have made transparent to life's deeper truth, the years fall away as destructive agents.

For the changeless beauty of this joy is not at war with time whose artistry life needs to draw out its infinitely various and subtle graces. Some of these graces may seem to contradict each other, youth's ardour and impetuosity, for example, seeming to challenge the repose of age. But because they spring from the same timeless root, they can grow together and in uniting, complete each other. The flame that burns unquenchably in the heart of life fulfils itself in the light of a loving awareness and to deny the flame, in whatever small degree, is to dim the radiance of the light.

For essentially life is in perfect agreement with itself, however variously it seems to manifest on different levels. This ordered constancy of being is the foundation of all trust and is reflected in every human loyalty. It persists through all the disconcerting phases and changes of existence and is revealed, too, in the meeting of extremes which proves that time is not a line which carries us ever further from our source, but a circle, of which the circumference is always equidistant from its centre and along which we travel, in rising spirals, to discover our beginning in our end and our end in our beginning. Even in looks the infant is old as well as new and the aged who have lived faithfully awake to the wonder of a second childhood.

For always we are meant to grow and it is only because our conception of growth has been limited to the body or because we have recoiled from the pains or commitments involved in enlarging the frontiers of our being that our spiritual arteries harden with our physical. We are meant to *grow* old just as vitally as we once *grew* up. Youth differs from age in possessing or being possessed by a physical vitality which, however enviable it may be in the eyes of the old, it is folly to try and preserve since increasingly it exacts more than it rewards. The young may squander the life of which they are imperfectly conscious. They may, fruitfully or disastrously, sow wild oats in the field of experience, since, for a while at least, they have rich reserves to draw upon.

It is less obvious that the old have vast resources too, since a new awareness is required to discover them. Such awareness is costly. It is not easy to be utterly loyal to life, when life has ceased to press its gifts with a smile upon us, when, indeed, it may well seem to have betrayed us, to be a pain which is hard to bear or a problem which we cannot solve or a flower which has withered in our hand. How fatally easy it is then to falter in our acceptance, to repudiate the hidden intention of life which needs exactly these untoward or daunting circumstances to quicken a new awareness by which life of a finer quality may reach us on a new level. Spiritual growth is arrested, at least for a time, at any point where this creative purpose is, for one reason or another, denied, and so a necessary readjustment between life and our evolving consciousness fails to take place. A blockage occurs, which will have to be removed before growth can freely continue and life circulate.

This failing to reach out to new sources of energy and to open up channels through which it can flow is associated in many people with the mistaken belief that we draw our vitality only from our roots in earth. This is to reduce the boundless adventure of living to what can be at best a heroic, at worst a pathetic, struggle against death.

In all of us, of course, the tide of physical life imperceptibly turns and more and more we feel its ebb. People differ greatly, too, in physical capacity and in the kind of vitality which, even in youth, they habitually expend. But even when it flows most strongly, it contains within it intimations of the super-physical, which tell us that the body is less a dynamo of atomic or animal energy than an organ upon which the spirit can play a music, crude or subtle according to the nature of the instrument, but a new variation in each one of us of the song which the stars sing together in the ever-renewed and renewing dawn of creation. And if its first music is that of the singing senses and of limbs that leap and dance, its last may be of a wisdom which finds at the heart of all change and movement the peace of a perfect meaning, that redeems the apparent treachery of time.

2

The sense of well-being enjoyed by a healthy body and continually renewed in the deeps of sleep is for many people the unconscious foundation of their faith in life and one for which they may well be grateful. Nor is it surprising if those who have known the zest of unreflective living and the joy of simple sensuous experience should cling to its diminishing returns as long as they can. For it does reflect an elementary unity of being which those who have awakened to self-consciousness and its complexities may well be tempted to envy.

Yet to cling to life at whatever level of experience is a fatal error. We dishonour Nature by limiting her generosity to the gift of instinct or even of intelligence. She has other gifts to offer, including and transcending these, in which we may receive more fully the total gift of herself that she intends. To attach ourselves to the body is to seal the well of life within us against the springs which replenish it from above as well as below. Most of us, less well-endowed with muscle and sinew, must have known genial giants of the flesh, who in the hey-day of their manhood lived masterfully in the world of material things. Then, in middle age, there came into their eyes that look of the bewildered child, the cornered animal and, eventually, of the poor old dog. The body in which they had invested all their faith had failed them and, lacking any other spiritual resource, they could only wait to die, sinking ever more deeply, if life should be kind to them, into the somnolence which is the body's habitual state when no demand, physical or spiritual, is made upon it.

Few today, however, even among those whose work is manual, are exclusively engrossed in the body. Indeed the manual worker who practises a true craft, exceptional as he may now be, is usually skilful in the craft of life and pursues perfection as a goal that can never be reached. Such a man would recognize the truth which Emily Dickinson so succinctly stated when she wrote, "we don't get older with the years, just newer" – newer because nearer to the original which we truly are, but which we need time, devotion and detachment to discover.

Yet in the rush of modern life it is all too easy to be

engulfed in a world of ageing adolescents who shrink from the hazard of growing up or are in too great a fever of mental or mechanical movement to study and practise its unhurried rhythm. This is the "strange disease" with its "sick hurry, its divided aims", which Matthew Arnold divined a century ago, because he felt it so painfully in himself and which made him regret so poignantly a time when "the sea of Faith was at the full".

> But now I only hear
> Its melancholy, long, withdrawing roar,
> Retreating, to the breath
> Of the night-wind, down the vast edges drear
> And naked shingles of the world.

The ancient world of which he lamented the passing may have been more of a dream than a fact. But it touched his heart. The world struggling to be born, for which he laboured as a champion of "sweetness and light", was at best but a forlorn hope. It is hardly surprising, then, that one so given to the backward glance, so haunted by a nostalgia for the irrecoverable, should, in a poem entitled "Growing Old", have traced his passage through life as a journey in which the living man changed, step by step, into a "hollow ghost", dead at last to all feeling of his total loss.

To sentimentalize over the past is an indulgence common enough among the ageing. And Matthew Arnold's cry of decrepitude was, perhaps, as much the protest of a body tired and a mind dispirited by a long routine of public service as a confession of inner frustration. Yet the spiritual *impasse* which he felt in himself and saw in his age has remained. The sickness which he diagnosed has become more virulent and the culture which, with so much earnestness and irony, he offered as the only alternative to an anarchy of tastelessness and ignorance, was itself too effete to rejuvenate a world intent on the pursuit of material power and its perquisites and so heading for its own destruction.

In our own century two distinguished poets have confronted the same spectre. T. S. Eliot might, indeed, be regarded in some ways as the Matthew Arnold of a later day, when the promised Utopia of mechanical progress had already become a "waste land", devastated by war within and without. No one has exposed the anatomy of that waste land more wryly than he or evoked more pungently the odour of its decay. But, for me at least, his thoughts, even when conforming to a traditionally Christian pattern, are too much, like those of his Gerontion, the "thoughts of a dry brain in a dry season", and as such unable to renew the springs of life.

"He has," wrote AE, "no light in his mind," and minds of such critical acuteness can seldom venture, spiritually, into the unknown. Yet by nothing less can we continue to grow. Eliot, like Arnold, can only cling with a mind chastened, but not really humbled even in his moods of "Ash Wednesday" contrition, to a culture and a creed of a kind to solace but not transform the disillusioned. Moving as his "Four Quartets" often are, they reflect a view of human life crippled with sin rather than quickened with a vision of its divine potentialities. The whole world, in his own words, "is our hospital" and he treads its wards like some shrewd but old-fashioned consultant, resigned to the perpetual presence of an incurable disease. In T. S. Eliot's "literary" and "ethical" religion the light of metaphysical or mystical insight at best but faintly glimmers. If there is any new wine here, it is too bitter to the taste to renew the springs of hope in the wounded heart. And love, doubtless because of its moral disrepute, is not only never directly invoked, but is intellectually deprecated.

For such a poet age is understandably less of an opening to the light than a deepening of the shadows. How alike in tone to Arnold's "Growing Old", though so much subtler in texture, are, for example, these lines from "Little Gidding":

> *Let me disclose the gifts reserved for age*
> *To set a crown upon your life-time's effort;*
> *First, the cold friction of expiring sense*
> *Without enchantment, offering no promise*
> *But bitter tastelessness of shadow fruit*
> *As body and soul begin to fall asunder.*
> *Second, the conscious impotence of rage*
> *At human folly, and the laceration*
> *Of laughter at what ceases to amuse.*
> *And last, the rending pain of re-enactment*
> *Of all that you have done, and been; the shame*
> *Of motives late revealed, and the awareness*
> *Of things ill done and done to others' harm*
> *Which once you took for exercise of virtue.*
> *Then fools' approval stings, and honour stains.*
> *From wrong to wrong the exasperated spirit*
> *Proceeds, unless restored by that refining fire*
> *Where you must move in measure, like a dancer.*

To judge by this passage, life, for a sensitive and intelligent person, culminates in total disenchantment. Only in the last two lines, which echo a Canto in Dante's *Purgatorio*, is a possible alternative to defeat offered. But it is hard to believe that so "exasperated" a spirit and one so sunk in ashes of the past could take advantage of it. For of the true genius and ripe wisdom of age there is hardly a hint in this rueful reflection on man's bondage to the temporal world and his misuse of his own faculties.

Far more passionately than T. S. Eliot did W. B. Yeats lament the dying fire of sensual life. "An aged man," he wrote in "Sailing to Byzantium",

> *is but a paltry thing,*
> *A tattered coat upon a stick, unless*
> *Soul clap its hands and sing, and louder sing*
> *For every tatter in its mortal dress.*

STEPPING WESTWARD

For him the song of age, unlike that of youth, caught in "sensual music", was the song of "unageing intellect" which only the Masters of Wisdom could teach.

> *O sages standing in God's holy fire*
> *As in the gold mosaic of a wall,*
> *Come from the holy fire, perne in a gyre,*
> *And be the singing-masters of my soul.*
> *Consume my heart away; sick with desire*
> *And fastened to a dying animal*
> *It knows not what it is; and gather me*
> *Into the artifice of eternity.*

Both poets see in fire the purifying and transforming element in which the soul may be delivered from its attachment to the dying body. But Yeats, as a poet, was in no hurry to be so delivered. His railings against the physical disabilities of old age, however understandable, are curiously immature nor made less so by his frank admission in the lines:

> *You think it horrible that lust and rage*
> *Should dance attention upon my old age:*
> *They were not such a plague when I was young:*
> *What else have I to spur me into song?*

That a poet, too, of his stature and visionary experience, on hearing of the Steinach method of rejuvenation, should have at once hurried to London to undergo the very dubious operation casts a curiously pathetic light on the degree to which he had really made his own the traditional wisdom upon which he set such store.

In that wisdom age is reverenced as a shrine awaiting us on the path of life in which the light can glow ever more pure and constant. But the modern poet who has lost the art of spiritually transmuting his vitality

[83]

and expressing it on a higher level, can only cry with Dylan Thomas,

> *Do not go gentle into that good night,*
> *Old age should burn and rave at close of day;*
> *Rage, rage, against the dying of the light.*

To take a bellows to a sinking fire may make, momentarily, a vivid blaze. But the quality of its flame remains unchanged. Yeats, however, if he failed to resolve the feud between "undying intellect" and the "dying animal", did see in the journey from youth to old age a dramatic involvement of eternity in time which guaranteed at every stage the possibility of new growth and discovery, of becoming more intimately and inwardly aware of the mystery of being into which every living person is born and dies.

Primitive man, as I shall show in the next chapter, is intensely and often fearfully aware of this mystery. For him all life is clothed in it and there are few things which he may not invest with a sacred significance and reverence as embodying something other and more than itself. But the realm of the sacred and numinous has almost vanished for civilized man beneath the scrutiny of physical science. With it have gone not only a multitude of degrading superstitions, but a habit of communion with Nature as a spiritual organism with which man is called to co-operate consciously.

To grow old wisely, indeed to grow at all beyond the bounds of his earthly disposition, it is essential for man to make his peace with his own nature by discovering its hidden dimensions and learning to live in habitual recollection of them. All through his history this has been man's central problem which his religions have tried, at different levels and with varying success, to solve. Western man has quarrelled with Nature ever since he was Christianized despite his Master's declaration that a house divided against itself cannot stand. The self-confidence which has

impelled him to great material achievements has been
dogged by an underlying anxiety, an insidious sense of
sin, because he has acted in ignorance or defiance of what
is supernatural in his being.

Christian dogma has more often aggravated than ap-
peased this situation by its indictment of the "natural
man". But his champions have maintained the feud in
reverse. In their earth-attachment they have been as wary
of the supernatural faculties as a poacher of a game-keeper.
Yet such faculties are as much part of the great Nature to
which we belong as the sensuality by which such Neo-
pagans claim to preserve their primitive roots in life.

This illusory conflict between the natural and the supernatural is man-made. It reflects a painful transitional stage
in his development, the struggle necessary to an evolving
consciousness, between what is of earth in his nature and
what is of heaven, what is outward and what is inward,
and it becomes intense as he strives to transform his earthly
nature from within. Supernature and nature are two levels
of the one great Nature and man's destiny is to reconcile
them. Growing old can justify Browning's optimistic
forecast that "the best is yet to be", if it is dedicated to
this task. For it has opportunities and aptitudes for exploring the world within which are seldom granted to those
who, in the first half of their lives, are necessarily pre-
occupied with the world without. And it is when life
slackens on one level that transition to another level
becomes both possible and necessary, if the momentum of
life is to be renewed.

3

Physically the evening of life can be a time of increasing
disability. But if this is accepted without regret or resentment, it can actually help us to discover our spiritual
resources and a new perspective in which the physical is

seen in a truer light. For spiritually we are neither old nor young. Time cannot "wither us nor the years condemn". Crippling illness or constant pain can, indeed, demoralize. Yet the example of many who have suffered such afflictions creatively are a heartening proof of the primacy of spirit and its power to redeem, in those who can effectively evoke it, all but the worst bodily disasters.

Admittedly nothing can be done on the level of the flesh, as Gerard Manley Hopkins wrote:

> To keep at bay
> Age and age's evils, hoar hair,
> Ruck and wrinkle, drooping, dying, death's worst
>   winding sheets, tombs and worms and tumbling
>   to decay.

But physical decay is not in itself a tragic thing. It may even be a means of transcendence. And though old age is on the brink of death, it need not be diseased. We have all known old men and women who have preserved into their last years a kind of radiance of well-being comparable to that of early childhood, as if the veil between them and the pure spring of life had become thin and transparent.

This may be exceptional today in a civilization so adverse, in its agitated rhythm, to harmonious growth and one in which the preservation of life by medical science does nothing to raise its quality. Physical survival is valueless in itself and too often it can mean for modern man, if not spiritual death, at least a moribund condition in which life, anaesthetized by time or dulled by drugs and narcotics, has ceased to unfold any new meaning. This may, indeed, happen long before old age. For unless we begin to develop an inner life and to work on the problems which it raises in our early and middle years, we shall be unlikely to possess the necessary resources or inclination to do so later on.

Those who enjoy excellent physical health and engage

in outgoing activities are less likely to feel concern for the inner life than those of a predominantly introverted temperament. But only the extreme extrovert is so blind to the conflicting forces of his own nature that he merely inflicts them by projection on to other people. Most of us are, in different degrees, both inward-looking and outward-acting in our disposition and those who pour out their energies in the service of others, even if it be rather insensitively, will mature in self-knowledge, if more slowly, perhaps, than the more self-conscious. Only those who selfishly indulge or exploit their vitality find themselves in old age equally disabled for the life within and the life without.

Nevertheless Keats was expressing a profound truth when he wrote that "until' we are sick, we understand not". In the work of another poet of our own day, Rilke, sickness as a means of transmutation was a constant theme. Wisdom is born of joy as well as of sorrow, but certainly the happy extrovert has less inducement than the sensitive introvert to face the tragic implications of human life and less capacity for being at once engaged and disengaged.

Wisdom is born of this capacity and the ideal of old age cherished in all ancient civilizations was one of ripeness in such wisdom as a result of a fulfilled at-onement with the divine powers. This, it was, that guaranteed psychological and spiritual maturity. The way to wisdom in the modern world cannot, in essentials, differ from that trodden by the sages of antiquity, but it has to be found and pursued under far more distracting conditions, which themselves impose, outwardly at least, a more radical challenge than the men of old had to meet.

Perhaps Goethe, though he was much more than a supreme embodiment of the enlightened man of the world, as some have regarded him, was the last modern sage to ripen into wisdom with an unshaken confidence that there could be no lasting quarrel between Nature and human intelligence. Yet he shared to the full the tasks and struggles of his fellow men.

Goethe's relative immunity from the split consciousness of modern man may, indeed, link him with the future quite as much as with the past. His view that by immersing oneself attentively in natural phenomena one could "learn to think creatively in the wake of nature", may make him, as Charles Davy has suggested,* a forerunner of the kind of consciousness towards which humanity is groping and of the wisdom which the years may bring to those who learn the art of creative living. To "think creatively in the wake of nature" is to experience her consciously from within instead of merely observing and measuring her with detachment from without. But to do this we need to change our own nature profoundly.

In Goethe's day this did not seem so necessary to human survival as it is today. As a first step to this change it is imperative for all who hope to discover how they have transgressed against Nature to ask, at a certain point, "Am I the self I think I am?" To such genial humanists as Harold Nicolson such questioners are tiresome "malcontents" who "not only doubt the reality of existence but suffer panic moments when they doubt their own reality. 'Am I really I?' they ask themselves, and this question invariably arouses within them the twin passions of dread and despair."

Yet it was just this question which a great sage of modern India, Ramana Maharshi, made the key to a true release from the bondage of the unreal. The question "Who Am I?" cannot be answered by the ordinary mind. In that lies its unique value. For it strikes at the very heart of the delusion under which we ordinarily live and, if persistently asked and pressed home, can pierce the egoistic shell and make an opening into mystery through which a new

* In *Towards a Third Culture* by Charles Davy (Faber).

kind of awareness can be born. It forces us back to that unconditioned source of life and being in which the sense of "I" originated and from which all thought ultimately derives.

To live anew in that source is to awake from the dream-state of physical and mental habit, characteristic of the conditioned ego, to the informing presence of conscious-ness itself. In that presence compulsive thought and the feeling which generates it die and mind and heart regain their true at-onement as an infinitely sensitive organ of pure intelligence and imaginative love.

Such was the transformation which the Indian Master had experienced himself and invited his disciples to undertake. And obviously such self-questioning differs utterly from the kind of negative introspection which Harold Nicolson deplores. Yet the egoist who, like Sena-cour, Matthew Arnold's "Obermann", begins to doubt "the truth of his own identity" has taken the first faltering step on the path which leads to the discovery of what he truly is and is not. By doubting the reality of the "I" to which he has been for so long unquestioningly attached and of the conventional world which has hardened like a carapace around it, he has begun to break the spell of illusion under which hitherto he was living.

He may well feel at first that his hold on life has been thereby dangerously weakened, that he has ceased to have firm ground beneath his feet or that he has exposed himself to a flood of abstract speculation. He has been treading the quick-sands of a self-centred life for so long and has learnt to adjust himself so skilfully to its hazards that it alone seems to provide some measure of security. To abandon this "I" is to cease to strive for a security which is only to be found, moment by moment, in the acceptance of life's ceaseless mutations.

When first we find ourselves asking "Who am I?" particularly if some shock or disaster has jolted us out of our habitual complacence, we may well experience the dread and despair which Harold Nicolson attributes to all self-questioners. If so, we can be sure that we are still clinging to the self whose reality we have begun to doubt. But if, humbly and steadfastly, we continue to question, without straining after an answer or expecting it to be intellectually given, we shall find that our minds grow calm and unperturbed as they open to a new dimension. We are then in a condition to receive the true answer to our question by experiencing what is real in the depth of our being.

For our self-questioning is needed to make space in the soul where delusive dreams and dreads used to crowd. In this uncontaminated space, a new movement of spiritual life and growth can begin.

We are impelled to such questioning by a growing sense that we are getting nowhere either in ourselves or in our lives and that to accumulate more knowledge or more possessions of the kind we already have would leave us exactly where we are. To recover meaning we have to open to the unseen reality which is inside both us and the world that extends in time about us. This is the source of all wisdom and understanding. Divorced from it, the world and our restless activities in it are meaningless and cannot achieve meaning, however industriously we pursue them. But once we are in relation with it, there is not the smallest act or object which is not meaningful. To deepen our realization and expression of such meaning should be the task and delight of our later years.

4

The wisdom of maturity, then, begins in a disengagement from the bonds of the natural man who views life from the outside through his sensory faculties and from the standpoint of an illusory self. This should be made easier by the inevitable decline in our physical powers and even by painful experience of their insufficiency. As the lure of external things diminishes with our ability to exploit them for our pleasure, we are more ready to respond to the vibrations of an inner world, at once present in ourselves and subsisting in every person and object around us. The more devotedly we respond to this unseen dimension, the richer the mystery which will reveal itself to our inner eye.

The visible and tangible world, in the changeable image and sensation of which we were once so engrossed and which was distorted by the self-interest with which we viewed it, will then be seen to derive its reality from something which cannot be perceived by the senses. We shall awake to the truth that what we and others really are is hidden from the outward eye and can only be spiritually perceived. We begin to see the world from the inside outward.

This is not to say that we despise or neglect our physical senses. On the contrary they can now begin to serve us as never before. Instead of being allowed to reveal to us only what we want to see in the furtherance of our crude or elevated designs upon life, they are now free to be the organs, on their own level, of consciousness itself, of the pure insight which is eternally active in us when we have cast away the burden of our private wants and fears and need no longer be either on the offensive or the defensive in our relation with the external world.

Maturity begins when we give up the struggle, which has proved more exhausting than exhilarating, to preserve our independence and manipulate life from outside. With this submission life begins to re-create us, quickening the inner faculties which we have neglected or but casually cultivated. The more intensely we attend to these faculties and exercise them, the more sensitive and flexible they become, just as our physical capacities did in our youth.

Through our physical senses we come into vital contact with the outer world. Our spiritual senses unveil for us an inner world of finer substance and timeless value. But they, also, transfigure for us the familiar world of nature, illuminating it in depth.

For the world we live in is determined by the quality of our relationship with it, which in turn depends upon the degree to which we see into our own nature. The more exclusively we live in and through our physical senses or through the unawakened mind which reacts incessantly to what conditions it from outside and is, indeed, the reflex of this cumulative conditioning, the more mechanical is our world and the shallower our impressions of it. The materialist's view of life reflects such a shallow contact. But when inner perception awakes, a new world is revealed. For we begin to experience life through that which is unconditioned in ourselves.

This new dimension of being in which we feel that we eternally exist transforms our sense both of reality and of ourselves as blissfully lost and found in it. No longer do we react negatively to a world which we cannot trust. For we know that the heart of that world beats within our own breast, and that we are not only at one with it in expansive sympathy, but can act creatively within it by a power of insight and understanding which transcends the sensory order.

The soul which possesses these faculties of inner perception has its own finer body through which it makes contact with the substance of the inner world, and both the mystic and the psychic researcher have discovered the possibility of passing out of the physical body into this subtler vehicle of consciousness and, for short periods at least, of functioning in it independently.

But we do not need to have a gift for astral projection to know that we experience life on different levels and move backwards and forwards between the timeless centre in us and the temporal circumference. Any dedicated artist or writer will remember hours when his will and soul have been so wholly immersed in his creative work that all sense of bodily actuality or of the external world has vanished as completely as in sleep, but with the difference that he has been intensely awake in that inner realm.

In later chapters I hope to treat more intimately of this experience and of what it means to re-establish our lives in the silence of the unconditioned. To do so is to enlarge at once our range of perception. Consciousness, though invisible to the ordinary senses, is the one ultimately real principle in the Universe. It acts with mounting intensity through a series of interrelated bodies or sheaths, the finer of which penetrate the grosser. Each level of consciousness takes form in a body which corresponds to it, one form sliding imperceptibly into another. Of these forms the physical body is the most dense and its awareness the most limited. But by cultivating our inner perceptions and the moral qualities which belong to them we come into possession of a body of increasing sensitiveness, which, indeed, was always latently ours, but which will only reveal its powers and faculties as we concentrate our attention upon them.

The decline, then, of our physical capacity in middle-age and later need not be regarded as a melancholy loss, but rather as a sign that other capacities await development and as an inducement to exercise them. It has been said that we spend the first half of our life in learning to live and the second half in learning to die. This is certainly true in terms of the physical body. For in learning to die to our attachment to that body, we are learning to live in freedom in whatever grade of body our spirit may assume. The more purely we experience this freedom and the growing radiance of spirit when it manifests in a body more sensitive and responsive to it, the less will physical death confront us as a denial of life. Instead we shall see it as a fulfilment of the life which we have been devotedly living, in which the dread and unrest inseparable from physical attachment will have slowly dissolved.

In growing old we shall then have truly grown young, not in inexperience, but in the faith which has opened the door of our earthly minds, with their burden of fear and perplexity, to the innocence of the divine world, to that wisdom which is "more active than all active things: she passeth and goeth everywhere by reason of her pureness. For she is the brightness of the everlasting light: the unspotted mirror of the power of God, and the image of his goodness. . . . For after this cometh night: but no evil can overcome wisdom. Wisdom reacheth from one end to another mightily; and she ordereth all things sweetly."

This surely is the Goddess whom, in our later years, we should enthrone in our hearts and whose presence should shed a grace and benediction upon old age. For she is the Queen of Heaven, the "most gentle Lady", who for Dante was a well of eternal light, and in the contemplation of whose serene beauty the thirst of the soul for any lesser loves is ultimately quenched.

PART TWO

✿

Learning To Be

❊

CHAPTER FIVE

The Initial Act

1

During the last fifty years astronomers and their telescopes have been looking further and further into space and enlarging our knowledge of what seems to be an expanding physical universe. They differ in their explanations of what the telescopes tell, but they and the atomic physicists have been revolutionizing our conception of space, time and matter.

Meanwhile nothing comparable has been happening, at any rate publicly, in relation to the spiritual universe, though privately, among those devoted to research into the inner nature of man, much work is being quietly done. That such research should lead to results which cannot be profitably publicized lies in the very nature of the field in which the research is done. This field is that of human consciousness itself. It is the subjective field as distinct from the objective field upon which telescopes can be trained. Yet it is a field within the self which can be at once immediately experienced and viewed with objective detachment.

This is due to the nature of consciousness, as it manifests in man. He is a being who lives on many levels or planes, though for a long time he remains unconscious of some of them. And he possesses the faculty of extending consciousness from one level to another, as he evolves according to the inherent law of his being.

His knowledge, therefore, of the nature of the spiritual

[97]

4

universe grows or declines with his knowledge of himself. And since for a long time his attention has been directed outwards to the study of natural phenomena, with the aid of measuring instruments, it is hardly surprising if his insight into the spiritual world and its qualities should have markedly declined.

But the tide is turning. Man, once again, is beginning to look within and seeking to renew the relationship between the cosmos and himself which to primitive man was immediate and self-evident. We have, in fact, reached another turn of the spiral along which man evolves and this explains why people today are increasingly drawn to that world of myth and symbol and arcane ritual, explored by anthropologist and archaeologist, in which the primitive imagination was at home.

During the ages in which man has been striving to civilize himself he has found that each culture which he so industriously built up contained within it the seeds of its own decline and that the civilizing process itself, as it has developed in modern times, has involved him in certain fundamental losses which more and more threaten to outweigh the surface gains. For, in the process of mastering nature and exploiting her powers, he has found himself to be increasingly alienated from the depths of his own being, while the world of his contriving becomes more and more uniform for want of some organic inspiration.

This process has doubtless not yet reached its term. Indeed it is at this present moment reaching out for new worlds in space to conquer. And for many, who feed their minds almost exclusively upon the latest sensations provided for them by press and radio, heaven has become only an area of space to be subdued and overrun by high-powered machines.

How differently the primitive conceived it. For him the sky was a supreme hierophany, a realm in which the sacred rites of creation were enacted and which gathered earth to itself in a holy marriage. For archaic man heaven symbolized, in itself and through the gods with whom he peopled it, a transcendence and changelessness, which he felt to be inwoven into the texture of his own nature. And through the rhythm of sun and moon, to which he instinctively responded, and the starry pattern in which he divined an intelligible meaning related to himself, this transcendence became an immanent power in his life, both energizing and sanctifying his physical being.

So, too, he regarded the elements of water and of earth. Through them the divine expressed for him its dynamic aspect in the mystery of death and re-birth and in the varied rites associated with seasonal vegetation, of agriculture and procreation. For the primitive imagination all natural objects were sacred because they were felt to be inherent in a boundless and bounding whole. The tree, for instance, as Mircea Eleade has shown so well,* supremely exemplifies the comprehensive meaning which a truly religious intuition can find in a natural object.

To primitive man it was equally an image of the cosmos, as the tree of life, and a symbol of life's fertility. Yet such meanings only enhanced for him the reality of the tree itself as a form of nature. Similarly space and time were not divorced from the timeless and spaceless dimension in which they were felt to exist. In the enactment of every true rite the temporal was conceived as being redeemed or reconciled with the eternal. An effective rite was regarded as a recovered fragment of "original time". It was at once timeful and timely and timeless.

But, as Professor Eliade points out, the primitive man's instinctive belief that by repeating archetypal actions he could maintain his sense of the ever-present sacredness of place and time never led him to depreciate life on earth in favour of a "spirituality" of detachment from the world. He was too firmly rooted in the natural world

* In his *Patterns in Comparative Religion.*

and in his own physical being to separate heaven from earth. Each belonged to the other.

Yet evidently he divined that there were forces which threatened the unity in which he sensed his well-being to consist and which might curtail or even sever the current of spiritual power which was mediated to him through the natural world and fracture the instinctive wholeness by which he experienced nature imaginatively. His rituals were, thus, designed as much to protect him and his group against dangerous psychic forces as to maintain his spiritual energies.

The gulf between the sacred and the secular, as we should call it, a gulf which yawns so wide in our modern world that the sense of the sacred has almost atrophied, existed for arcane man as a hazard and a temptation against which appropriate action must be continually taken. Through his myths and initiation trials he reminded himself in dramatic form of the imaginative act required to maintain the spiritual and natural health of which he was the human trustee.

In this imaginative act the two dimensions of being and becoming, inherent in human existence, were brought together and, so long as he could harmonize them, he enjoyed a profound intuition of sharing, in whatever he did, in the total drama of creation. Hence his genius for reading the whole into every part, however small, of his daily life and for experiencing natural events as modes of being.

This, in briefest outline, was the universe, at once spiritual and natural, of archaic man when consciousness had begun to inform, without as yet subverting, his instinctive integrity. Today we cannot regain such a universe by any direct route. What to him was only a felt threat to wholeness of being has become for us a split in consciousness which only a new realization of what we are can redeem. To imagine ourselves back, with the help of archaeologists and anthropologists, in a primitive world is to return to our own childhood. At least, it was in childhood that we were nearest to it and most immune from the disruptive forces of modernity.

But we had to grow up, as did mankind. The gulf had to open; man was not meant to remain in what Keats called "the Infant or Thoughtless Chamber". Imperceptibly we are impelled by the wakening of the thinking principle within us, through the Chamber of Maiden Thought and all its pleasant wonders, into that arena where thought and life come to grips and the idealism of the heart is confronted by "a world full of Misery and Heart-break, Pain, Sickness and oppression", in which the spiritual light within is dimmed by the darkness without where "ignorant armies clash by night" and we seem to live, not in one world, but in two.

On the one hand, apprehended, if at all, in moments of withdrawal from the immediate demands of life, is a vast, calm, impersonal realm of spirit, perfect and remote. On the other is a world, that presses urgently upon us, of personal struggle for mastery, a world of antagonism and challenges and failures, of uneasy truces that merge into renewed conflict – the world in which, in confused fellowship with others, we strive to know and to forget ourselves.

This is the world of divided being and incipient awareness through which we all have to pass before we can hope to regain in full consciousness that sense of being natives of a universe, informed throughout with spiritual meaning and mystery, a cosmos which primitive man, despite his lack of specific mental development and his terror of the unknown, possessed on his own level as his natural birthright.

Doubtless, to many, caught in the fever and flux of the modern world, the idea that our greatest need is to reconsecrate life through being faithful to a deeper reality in ourselves can have little meaning. For their inner condition and their outer situation seem equally to deny the possibility. Yet though mythological man may seem remote, indeed, from mechanical man, so far as there is such a species, the sense of the sacred lies deep in the human heart. Life, indeed, may be profaned at many levels but it remains pure and whole at the core. And we have something more relevant to our modern environment than the records of archaic cultures to justify a faith that the self-consciousness which divides is only a phase in a process of spiritual evolution which can culminate, even here on earth, in a fullness of knowledge and being. For we have the words and the lives of the Masters, who have trodden the path which leads from a life at the mercy of the unreal to one which is centred in the real.

So long as we are divided in mind and heart, we cannot conceive or perceive the real. At most we can only catch glimpses, in our calmer and more reflective moments, of an order of life more true than what is habitually our own. Our sense of life and of ourselves can expand, quickened it may be by the words of a poet, by a work of art or a piece of music, or by some deed of unself-conscious goodness, which we witness or of which we hear or read. And in that moment of enlargement we will feel that there is a world of experience which would vastly enrich our life and transform its quality, could we enter and dwell in it.

Generally, however, such moments lead nowhere. Like happy dreams, they are at best the consolation of a waking life in which dreams can have no valid place. But the great Teachers of mankind have made the dream come true, have lived so faithfully that self-consciousness has ceased to be a partial faculty of thought and awareness and has found the whole to which it essentially belongs. In the light of their testimony and example it is our waking life which is the dream.

This, then, is the task which modern man is being

impelled to undertake. For Nietzsche was right in his view that Man is unfinished, though wrong in the kind of super-man he conceived. Primitive man, by religious rite and social custom, sought to preserve his natural integrity in a universe which he felt to be charged with spiritual power and meaning. Modern man can only become imaginatively whole by a profound act of inward re-creation. It is within that he has to rediscover and affirm the reality of a spiritual universe by uncovering his real humanity, which is also divine.

This inward exploration and the practices associated with it are a necessary condition of any true and humanly enriching relation with the outer world known to the senses and measured by the calculating mind. Man may increase his knowledge of the mechanism of the universe by throwing metal at the moon, but he will be little nearer understanding the nature of its mind or its heart. To come near to that he must, also, look patiently and dispassionately within. For what he finds there and what happens to him in the process of finding it will transform his vision of the world without.

In the pages that follow I shall try to suggest, as simply as I can, something of what this involves and of the creative pattern which an imaginative mind divines, alike in its own depths and in the cosmos of which it is a part.

2

Every creative adventure involves an act of faith. The scientist, working in the field of physical phenomena, calls this the acceptance of a hypothesis, which is put to the test of experiment and either verified or disproved. In the field of spiritual experience more than a mental supposi-tion is required. For here we need to commit ourselves to something which exceeds our mind's reach and which may even seem to contradict its findings. We must, of course, recognize these contradictions, but we are not yet in a condition to resolve them fruitfully, if that is possible, because we are divided in mind and so are ourselves in a state of inward contradiction.

We have to discover whether this state corresponds with the nature of things. Is such a condition native to life and necessary to its maintenance? Or is it an aberration peculiar to ourselves at this moment of time? If we rush to answer this question and begin to argue about it, we shall remain just where we were, taking one side or the other, but wholly convinced by neither. For in the spiritual field truth has to be lived to be known, and so, indeed, has falsehood.

The act of faith, then, required of self-conscious man is primarily an act of faith in life as a perfect whole despite all the apparent imperfections and schisms which seem to contradict such a belief. This is much more than an intellectual assent to a possible theory. For even if the knowledge he has acquired about the nature of life and the forces which hold it together lend support to such a theory, his heart has still to assent to it. Until it can do so, it matters not how much evidence he may gather which points to the oneness of the world, he will still contradict it in himself.

An act of faith is not a positive assertion about life, based on what seems to be sound evidence. No faith is required for that. It is rather a leap into the dark, not taken blindly or irresponsibly, but with a total readiness to experience life at a new depth. As such it is a spiritual act as distinct from a mental or an emotional one. In such an act, truly grounded in faith, the mind does not dominate the heart nor does the heart indulge its own reasons at reason's expense. Most of our acts are in some degree self-interested. In them we impose ourselves, helpfully or harmfully, on life and on other people, even if only negatively through indifference. We may intend well or ill. Our will may be activated more by an idea or by an emotion. But in either case it is partial and one-sided. For it reflects the bias of our personality, which has been mis-formed from without by the impact of life and people on us. And without an act of faith we cannot be re-formed from within by the Spirit which creates and re-creates us. Such an act differs from all the personality's wilful acts in expressing a willingness to serve a truth beyond our grasp with the whole of our being and, in serving it, to cease to desire that our views or beliefs should prevail over those of others or to know where this faith will lead us. Far from being neutral or non-committal such an act is one of total commitment.

But to what? Not, obviously, to the God of any exclusive doctrinal system, although some worshippers of such a God may be led on to apprehend the reality which Paul Tillich has called "the God beyond God". For a pure act of faith must be grounded in a Godhead which transcends any attempt of ours to define it, still less to claim for our definition a monopoly of truth. In all such attempts we have designs upon the Mystery instead of allowing It to unfold Its own form and meaning through us.

Pure faith is as innocent of credulity as of scepticism. It is rooted in humility and patience, in the readiness to wait and devotedly work, within and without, until the schism is healed between heart and head, instinct and rationality, subconscious impulse and self-conscious interest, which stultifies our thinking and our living. Only thus can the Truth which is the informing genius of life enlighten and resolve our discord. However impossible it may seem and is for our divided nature to compass such an act of faith, we can, in time short or long, consent to it and put our consent into practice. Then re-creation and re-integration can begin.

Experience, however, shows that hitherto few have fully consented to it, until every other plausible way out of their predicament was blocked. And this, with few exceptions, is as true of those who profess a religious belief as of unbelievers. For creative faith differs in kind from the willed belief which creeds so often fortify. It involves a readiness to allow life to unfold its meaning as we grow into deeper conformity with its inner truth. And since belief and unbelief are half-truths of the unenlightened mind, each is a necessary and balancing ingredient of experience until we have begun to live the truth which includes and goes beyond both.

In committing ourselves to a reality which we cannot hope to comprehend in any series of definitions, but only to image and express in the degree of our fidelity to it, we reject nothing which reality includes. All that we are, with our questioning minds, our impulsive hearts, our assertive wills, our pleasure-loving and pain-resenting senses, we offer to the Power which creates and re-creates us, and which we can feel as life or seek as truth or worship in generous, self-forgetful moments as love.

But that may well seem to be just what we cannot do. Our self-centred condition is a perpetual reminder of our incapacity and of a bondage to warped notions and habits which we cannot throw off. Yet at least we have become conscious that such bondage is a sickness of soul and a diminishment of life. And the more sensitive we are to its consequences in ourselves and upon others, the more urgent is our longing to find a way out.

This is what brings many people today to the psychologist, and for some the therapy which he can offer may be a helpful preliminary to the journey which we are meant to undertake. Indeed the more advanced stages of this therapy belong to the initial stage of the journey itself, as I have already suggested. For the "deep centre" which is the quest of Jungian psychology is nothing else than the Soul of our being, as the title of one of C. G. Jung's books, *Modern Man in Search of a Soul*, explicitly declares. As

[106]

such it is the quest of every religious faith. There is only one miracle in the world, that of being reborn from division into wholeness. And whether the technique by which this is made possible is called psychological or religious or neither, its object is to remove the obstacles which prevent this perennial miracle from occurring, moment by moment, on every level of our being.

Evidently in this age the relentless grip of the anxious mind can be loosened in some by the alchemy of dream-analysis. The deeps may be opened and the initial act of faith accomplished in this way, as in others by the repetition of a *mantra* or invocation. But even those who take this way successfully would admit that they have only started upon the journey into that Self which they truly are. They have made conscious contact with their unconscious or super-conscious source and its creative forces on one level. But on others they are relatively unawakened and untested.

The act of faith by which the deeps of our being are fully opened to the regenerating power of life and we become experiencing souls can, in fact, in this age as in others, be accomplished along the traditional path of the ancient wisdom. It has not been outdated for those who are ready to tread it devotedly, though it may need to be re-stated. Human nature, now as ever, is seldom ready to do this until life has chastened it. And though psychology may weaken some of its resistance and even dethrone the ego in which this resistance is centred, the experience of all who have set out on this journey and faithfully pursued it shows how far from final dissolution the separative self can be even in men and women who, in knowledge of its requirements, are far upon the way.

Certainly no initial act of faith, whether accomplished by psychological means, by a voluntary surrender from within or by conversion engendered from without, can wholly transform our natures. We are still, in parts of our nature, enveloped in the ignorance which we are meant to outgrow. The conflict of heart and mind is eased but not fully resolved. This I have had to learn painfully myself in a life largely devoted to striving to heal the wounds suffered in early years.

But once we have achieved the initial movement of faith, we are no longer insulated from the possibility of spiritual growth. Just as when we take a seed from the florist's packet and sow it in the soil, we can find the seed of true being waiting to shoot and flower in us and entrust it to the mysterious Power within. Nor need we do this blindly. Knowingly we can commit ourselves to That Which exceeds our knowing and resolve to maintain this act of faith by continually deepening our awareness of what it means and of what happens to us as a result of it. We have entered the "Sacred River" of which an Indian sage wrote:

> The Spirit in thee is a river. Its sacred bathing place is contemplation; its waters are truth; its banks are holiness; its waves are love. Go to that river for purification; thy soul cannot be made pure by mere water.*

The action of creative faith, if it is sustained in the face of all that would deny and thwart it, will cleanse us in the process of changing and transforming us. But to be cleansed of what is unreal or perverse in thought, feeling and will is inevitably a testing experience and generally the trial is prolonged and often marked by unexpected and what may seem undeserved set-backs. That, however, is true of every vital and authentic commitment.

And what sustains the soul, dedicated to discovering and living its own truth, and helps us to bear the aches and toils and hazards of the way, is the inward sense, slight and variable as it may often be at first, of being in intimate touch with Something infinitely more real than our harassed

* From the *Hitopadesa*. Tr. from the Sanskrit by J. Mascaró.

personality. There are still the stresses on the surface. Indeed they may well seem to have been intensified. But now, by this act of unwilful faith, we are aware of being related to a mysterious Power which comprehends and can reconcile in Itself all the diverse forces which still dispute for sovereignty over our outer nature. In other words we have acknowledged the basic ground of our being in which our divided faculties can find their common root and enter into concord. And through doing this we begin to see and love the inward truth of things, which does not depend on what the outer senses tell us, but illuminates them.

A true act of faith, then, re-creates the cosmos within us and our vision of the cosmos without. We re-enter the spiritual universe which primeval man instinctively knew. But we re-enter it with a self-awareness born of humanity's long struggle with an objective world, which qualifies us to become conscious free-men in a universe to which primitive man was relatively bound by the limited reach of his instincts.

Primitive man looked outward and saw the physical world as a spiritual realm in which he intimately participated as a physical being. In this respect and on this level his vision was incomparably truer than our own. But his experience of an inner world, independent of the physical universe, though intimately related to it, was elementary. He had hardly begun to look within himself. When he did, the spell under which he lived in the embrace of mother Nature was broken and he had begun the long, painful journey to adult manhood.

Today we know a good deal about that long journey, as we look back over the stormy surge of human history, strewn with the apparent wastage of its implacable feuds. But there is a credit side to the account of man at war with himself. There are the glories of creative genius, the victories of the human mind, in every realm of thought and practice, over ignorance and superstition, and the graces, however exceptional, of pure goodness, of a goodness in which the instinct of the natural man has become infused with a light that transcends the elementary order of nature.

We need to remember these achievements of the human spirit today, when we may be tempted and are, indeed, urged by some revolutionary voices to repudiate the cultural tradition of the past. To cling to that past is certainly fatal to new growth. The humanism of the last three hundred years, in so far as it was a creed, has had its day. For it was tainted with privilege and came to live too much on the spiritual capital of the past. But the sensibility which it nurtured, the imagination which it trusted and the intellectual and moral range of its vision, before it declined in these latter days into a kind of scientific rationalism, live on in its greatest works to strengthen our faith in man's creative resources.

Nevertheless, in this age when men and women, on every social level, are awaking, prematurely it might often seem, to the temptations and hazards of self-consciousness, and when the world that science has manufactured threatens to kill the nerve of creative living, there is a need of something much more potent than an educative study of the art and learning of the past or the virtues of a liberal outlook.

"That the visible world is part of a more spiritual universe from which it draws its chief significance," was the first conclusion which William James drew, early in this century, from his study of varieties of religious experience. Few today, however, would admit to possessing any direct knowledge of that spiritual universe or recognize as their essential vocation the bending of their human faculties to the task of infusing spiritual meaning into the physical world, from which their bodies are sprung.

Yet this is our distinctive role in the creative drama in

which we play, here on earth, a central part. And even when we perform that role perversely, exploiting or manipulating the powers of nature for our own delusive advantage, we only prove how impossible it is to escape our responsibility. For there is no power in life but spirit and to possess it consciously endows man with as awesome a capacity for unlimited destruction as for divine creation.

The universe will reveal its spiritual form to us when we are ready and able to see it through being ourselves spiritually changed. Admittedly, to the visionary eye, the pattern of the physical universe which the atomic physicist and biochemist are disclosing today is wonderfully suggestive of the nature of the creative genius informing life on other planes than the physical and phenomenal. But interesting as it is to know that the Sun functions as a celestial atomic pile or that life, if born of and nurtured by earth, descends from above as air and light to quicken into being the whole world of vegetation upon which man and animal depend, such knowledge cannot restore to us that inherent sense of oneness with the Cosmos which primitive man possessed.

To describe nature, our own or that of the Cosmos, is not to experience her. To regain our vision of life as a consecrated whole, of which we are meant to be joyous devotees, we have to begin life afresh, depending on no outside tool or instrument. We have to entrust ourselves to the creative spirit, inherent in life on every level of its manifestation, where it rests and works unseen in the depths of our being. What once we did unconsciously and still do to the extent that we exist as bodies, we have now to accomplish consciously.

Throughout the childhood and youth of the individual or the race such a conscious act is necessary only in a minor degree. The body grows and the mind unfolds its powers up to a certain point, obedient to the genius of life within it, though environment and education may help or hinder the working of that genius.

But when the natural faculties have fully developed and the individual is in some sort of possession of them, he is faced with a critical choice. He may accept the range of experience which they offer him and continue to live within its limits, guided mostly by self-interest, modified in different degrees by the morality of his time and place. He will then cease to grow, as a vital and sentient organism. He may not deteriorate morally if he is a responsible and orderly person, but he will cease to develop spiritually. And a society composed of people, few of whom are growing spiritually, will before long degenerate. No longer deeply rooted in or obedient to natural law, it will lose its instinctive direction and, with that, the principle of unity which held it together. The same thing will happen, of course, with most of the individuals who compose it. Indeed, that is, in many ways, the condition of Western man today.

This, then, is the moment when the critical choice has to be made. Can we collaborate with life in a new way, consciously and willingly? For this is what life requires of us, if our spiritual faculties are to unfold as healthily as our physical powers did in childhood and if we are to realize the full potentialities of the human state. Should we fail to do this, life in us is arrested and congealed between two states of being, to neither of which we can wholly assent and which can only be reconciled at a deeper level to be discovered in ourselves.

In the universe known to our sense the sun is the centre of a planetary system of which our earth is a part. All the life and growth of nature depend upon it. And if we are to believe the ancient teachings, the cycles of development through which humanity has passed since it first emerged as a unique species on this globe have been symbolically represented, if not occultly determined, by the movement of the sun through the twelve signs of the Zodiac. Consequently from time immemorial the sun has been worshipped both as the radiant fount of life and, symbolically, as the heavenly Lord of our being.

In the imagination of ancient poet and seer it was not only a great vortex engendering heat, but a spiritual sphere from which myriads of Angelic beings radiated light and power into the hidden depths of man's soul, enabling him to ascend out of the ignorance of his animal nature towards the realm of wisdom and love which was his true home.

Doubtless few modern astronomers, if asked what they saw when they observed the sun rising, would exclaim with William Blake: "I see an innumerable company of the Heavenly host crying 'Holy, Holy, Holy is the Lord God Almighty'." But that does not disprove the truth of Blake's vision. Looking *through* and not *with* his corporeal eye, he saw the sun as it shone in the heaven of his heart and as the regenerating principle of his spiritual faculties. Of this inward sun the outer sun, apparent to the physical senses, was an image. But it, also, performed the same central function in the physical universe as that hidden sun, which his imagination conceived, performed in the universe of his subjective being.

There was a profound correspondence between them. But only the man of new vision could see the physical sun as a spiritual orb, its outer splendour being but a reflection of the glory within. As Blake so perfectly put it: "To the Eyes of the Man of Imagination, Nature is imagination itself. As a man is, so he sees."

Primitive man possessed this imagination. He was a natural seer. But in him self-consciousness still slept. In most of us self-consciousness has killed or at least maimed the faculty to see things whole, which is what creative vision is. But we have earned thereby the possibility of being distinctively ourselves, of realizing the truth of our individual being and living it, as no primitive intelligence could. To do this, we need to take the inward path which will eventually bring us into a new and free relation with the outer world of nature and of man.

The initial act of faith commits us to this path, which, though dark at first and often leading us later through dark places, is lit by a hidden sun, that sun of which the *Isha Upanishad* declares:

The face of Truth is covered by a golden disk. Uncover it, O Lord of light, that I, who love the true, may see.

CHAPTER SIX

✲

Entering the Silence

1

Many of us must have known moments of inner silence, moments when thought and memory have ceased and self-will has relaxed its efforts to isolate us from the universal life in the little cramped and cluttered cell which we have made our own. It may have been only for an instant, but in that instant we have been nothing and needed nothing. We have slipped back to the beginning when we allowed life or God, or whatever we like to call the Power which brought us into existence, to do the willing and the thinking for us.

Such momentary relapses into an infantile condition bear but a superficial likeness to the "return to origin" of which the mystics speak. Yet in the first stages of that return something very similar has to happen. It differs from the chance and involuntary letting-go that the stress of life imposes upon us, as a respite from long-sustained effort or unbearable tension, in being consciously chosen in the conviction that only so can we recover the inspiration and direction of a Will greater than our own.

Even so it may be long before we can reach the depths in which we really begin to experience the Silence, still less to express it. I shall be discussing later some of the means by which, according to traditional teaching, the initial hindrances, represented by our ingrained habits of resistance to the surrender required of us, may be reduced. Here I am assuming that either faith or the

[115]

painful compulsion of life itself have brought us to the point when, for brief periods at least, we make a practice of crossing the threshhold of silence in the hope that it will have something to say to us.

At first, in such times of withdrawal from the noisy but fascinating world that engrosses our senses, we may feel lost in a featureless limbo. For most of us life exists primarily through our relation to an external universe and, so far as we are conscious of ourselves, it is largely through our relationship with other people or with a world of objects, animate or inanimate. This is, of course, what life at a certain level intends. It is the partial but practical relation which we had to develop, slowly and with considerable difficulty, from the beginning when, as infants, we were dropped into this strange world. And we have gone on doing so with more or less skill and aptitude ever since, becoming increasingly self-conscious and differentiated from our surroundings in the process.

So it is hardly surprising if, when we voluntarily deprive ourselves of this external reference, we should feel lost. Of course we deprive ourselves of it in sleep and to some extent in periods of vacancy while we are awake. But such vacancy is generally a condition in which we are unaware of the vacancy itself or only aware of it as a vague background to drifting thoughts or images which our mind has ceased to focus.

To enter the inner world differs from this condition in so far as our intention is to remain as alert in this subjective realm as we like to think we are in the world of people and things. Inevitably we fail at first to sustain our intention. To empty our minds is difficult enough. To continue conscious of nothing and yet attentive is beyond our powers for more than a few seconds. Our old habits are too strong for us. They insist that we must cling to something, if we are not to fall into the abyss, and there is no lack of thought-forms ready to supply our need.

[116]

ENTERING THE SILENCE

We may close our eyes against the outside world, but our brains are full of images which that outside world has impressed upon them and of notions or incidents which are in the forefront or the background of our memory. We do not need to summon them. They form the grain and tissue of that transitory but tenacious self which we suppose ourselves to be. Only as that self dissolves do they lose their power over us. The tyranny they still exert when we try to maintain an inner silence shows how far we are as yet from wholly desiring the dissolution of that self. To drift with life and the shallow currents we have set up in it is so disastrously easy; to live with sensitive awareness so endlessly hard.

Yet it is for that purpose that we enter the inner world. What we intend is that we should cease to exist as entities whose activities are to a large extent mechanically determined from without because of our inward insufficiency, and that, by finding our hidden reality we should ultimately succeed in transforming our relationship to the outer world from a state of bondage to one of freedom and intimate understanding. Then, instead of reacting helplessly to the surface of life, as it assaults or allures us, we shall meet its forces from a centre of true Self-recollection, an eye of being within us, which sees through and beyond life.

To succeed in this aim, we have to learn to allow the inner world to reveal itself to a faculty in us which is not disturbed by the fever and fret, the excitements or ambitions in which we are superficially entangled. Since we are largely unconscious that we possess such a faculty and at best have used it so little, this is obviously a most difficult undertaking. Without a reversal of wilful habits we could never accomplish it. Those who have accomplished it agree in declaring that an important key to eventual success is to be found in an abandonment of all desire to succeed. For it is the interested motive implicit in such desire which stultifies every attempt to be pure in heart and mind. What is required is a new kind of act to which the whole of us consents. Our habitual self is incapable of such an act. It is equally partial when it acts or refrains from action. Cramped by self-consciousness, we cannot yield to that mysterious Power in the depths of our being in which positive and negative meet. Nor consequently can we fully lose and find ourselves in the objects which attract us. We can only possess or be possessed by them. To get inside anything, we have to get outside our habitual personality.

The act which we have to learn to perform, if we are to bring the outer and inner world into true relation, requires that we should cease to attach ourselves to things through the sensations, feelings and thoughts which they excite in us. Hitherto people and things, with rare exceptions, have existed for us less in their own right than to gratify us or feed our self-esteem. This is the measure by which we have tended to value them, which is equally unfair to the object and impoverishing to ourselves. Indeed such an attitude, if carried to an extreme, would reduce the whole world to a mere projection of our appetite for power, pleasure or prestige.

We can never correct this bias by enlarging our appetite or denying it. The flaw is not in our natural faculties but in our misuse of them. Only by finding the kernel of true being in ourselves and by grounding our life in it can we enter into communion with the true being in everything else. It is to find this hidden kernel that we invoke the Silence. And the Silence becomes real to us as we cease to identify ourselves either pleasurably or painfully with our feelings and thoughts. Only then can we become fully aware of them and calmly maintain this awareness. In that moment of watchful, disinterested awareness we are freed from their compulsion. Such attentiveness transforms a merely negative letting go into a releasing act.

The tighter we are bound by selfish habits, the harder it

will be at first to maintain this loving attentiveness even momentarily. But as we develop some skill in loosening the knot which habit has tied, we find that the disturbing inrush of images and thoughts has less power to subdue us to itself. The stream of life and change will always flow until time, if ever, has an end. We cannot dissociate ourselves from that stream, as distinct from our wallowings and flounderings in it, even if we would. What we need to learn is the art of flowing freely and harmoniously within it at a selfless depth, experiencing life purely from moment to moment without distorting anticipation or regretful after-thought.

To achieve this we need to discover what is timeless in ourselves, to know it as eternally real, and to experience all life in and through it. This is the root of our being, the divine unity in which all conflict is resolved. We turn to the Silence because we instinctively know that we are nearer to this essence of our being when we are still and receptive than at any other time and that until we have learnt to open our hearts to it and to keep them open, false tension in thought and act will continue to demoralize us.

Eventually, when we have succeeded in being empty and still for longer and longer periods, we can contemplate this emptiness and wait for it to reveal as much of its nature as we have the vision to see. By allowing what seems at first to be unreal, because it lacks familiar form and definition, to permeate our being, we begin to feel in It something incomparably more real than any external fact and, in ourselves, a quality of life which is new and unanalysable. For the Void, as Buddhists call it, is not definable in terms of space and time. It is what we are and the world is when we cease to crave or cling to anything transitory.

The scientists have, indeed, told us that emptiness is the norm of the physical universe, that a solid is chiefly holes and so is the air we breathe, the water we drink, and the body in which we live. The mystics say the same in their own language. Meister Eckhardt, for example, remarked that when things are useful, it is that in them which is Nothing which makes them useful. And Lao-Tzu said: "Thirty spokes meet the axle, but the utility of the wheel is in the space between them. We make vessels of clay, but their true nature is in the emptiness within. We cut out doors and windows to form a house and it is on these spaces where there is nothing that the house depends." All the forms of life which the universe contains exist in a matrix of apparently empty space without which they could not be. Nothing, in the physical universe, is the overwhelmingly necessary condition of something. Increasingly we realize that it fulfils the same function in the spiritual universe which we have begun to explore.

But reality in the inner world which we have entered, cannot be measured by the mind of physical science. It is a world of quality, not quantity, which has to be felt and valued directly. It will reveal itself to us as all mental and emotional hindrances to integral awareness fall away. When one can apprehend what is behind thought, said a Buddhist sage, one is on the way to wisdom. It is for this that we wait and work. And little by little or, it may be, suddenly, our patience and attentiveness will be rewarded. Our awareness of Nothing will begin to quiver with a life of its own, instinct with a quality which we had rarely, if ever, experienced before. We may call it a peace which is other than a sensation of quiet or a cessation of noise, a peace so potent that no sensation can disturb it, because it rises in us and enfolds us from a realm of being beyond the world of change.

This ineffable peace is likely to be the first direct intimation we have of the timeless dimension in which we live all unconsciously even when we are mentally engulfed in the world of restless movement. But amid the noise and agitations of that world we have lost touch with the hidden depths of ourselves. We cannot regain them so long as there is unrest in our hearts or minds. But as we allow this to die away and the pool of meditation becomes calm and clear, we begin to realize the presence of Something which contains and surpasses us, to sense in the ground of our being a reality to which nothing is alien or unloved but which cherishes in Its silent heart all the ever-changing forms which image Its changeless being. This reality is no abstraction. It is as palpable to our spiritual senses as the air our bodies breathe. For the chatter of our minds, pursuing notions, as hounds pursue their quarry, is still.

It is then as if we had regained the silence from which our first word came when, as little children, we struggled to give shape to sound. All the words which, since then, our minds have devoured and multiplied and through which the living truth has become more and more diluted and verbalized, are swallowed up in a moment of naked being. We may wish later to name the presence which is Silence itself the better to relate ourselves to It and to articulate Its mystery. But the Silence has taught us that it is immeasurably beyond any name which men have given to It and any form in which imagination may clothe it. Though present in every form, we shall know that no form can contain It, least of all our own, that transient vessel of life in which our spirit strives to distil the essence with which this perfect Presence endows it.

2

The intensity of this experience will vary with the degree of silent awareness to which we have attained. But to know this peace from beyond the boundaries of the finite is likely to be the first step in the liberation of the soul from its ignorant attachment to the world of the senses. It is the ground in which the new kingdom of a soul-centred life can begin to grow. Previously we may have had ecstatic moments in which we lived beyond ourselves and felt the breath of the infinite. But because they were not grounded in this inward peace, the ecstasy of spirit was tainted with vital excitement.

By contrast the silence which now invades and envelops us stills all vital unrest, penetrating into the very cells of our body as well as dissolving all the cares and anxieties which have burdened our mind. So blessed is our relief from habitual tension that we may well be tempted to regard this as the goal of our seeking instead of the foundation upon which we are required to build. But even if it were possible to return again and again to this condition for rest and renewal, we should never be more than spiritual convalescents. In the haven of quietism we may gather strength and learn to adjust ourselves to the new rhythm which the Silence is inducing in our hearts. But we must not linger in it too long.

Above all we must not lose our human bearings or disown our commitments in the actual world, although these commitments may well change their nature in correspondence with the change in ourselves. The dangers attendant on all who set out to enlarge and deepen the human condition are too well known and have been too often exemplified to need stressing. The only sure safeguard against them is purity of motive and a true dedication to a task in which self-will and self-seeking can have no place, a dedication to be continually reaffirmed as being the essence of the act of self-surrender to which we are committed.

Our only will is to become truly responsive to a creative power which is not our own but which wills to make us its own. That power will be perfectly adapted to our receptive capacity at any given moment, provided we are really humble and sincere in our aspiration. But if, in invoking this power, we are in any way presumptuous in mind or acquisitive in will and feeling, we shall not embody the genius and grace of spiritual understanding, but display some form of monomania, fanatical or eccentric. The two conditions are utterly other, but in the tortured religious history of mankind they have been often confused, with disastrous consequences.

Another error into which we may fall when we are new to this experience of the non-self is to recoil from our individuality as if it were opposed to the universality in which we long to merge. But true individuality which the outgrowth of "personality" stifles, is a distinctive expression of the universal and represents the principle of unique being with which every sentient creature is endowed. All the rich diversity of life is a flowering of this principle. And, unless we are true to it, we cannot enter into the dance of life and of mutual awareness, in which we strike fire from each other. It is because our awareness has lost its roots in true being and has become conventionally hide-bound that we experience life so poorly whether we are by temperament solitary or gregarious. But as we immerse ourselves in the Silence, we draw nearer to that greater Consciousness which creates us in the likeness of Itself and knows Itself in us. Of this restoration in the self of the ideal principle of things the fifteenth-century mystic, St Peter of Alcantara, wrote: "Let a man return into his own self, and there in the centre of his soul, let him wait upon God, as one who listens to another speaking from a high tower, as though he had God in his heart, as though in the whole creation there was only God and his soul."

The neophyte in the temple of the soul has to learn to listen before he can hope to hear. The "sensual ear", as Keats called it in a famous Ode, has to give place to the spiritual ear and until we have begun to hear with it and to develop, too, a faculty of spiritual vision, we may well seem to have lost all identity and all capacity in Something immeasurably other than ourselves. As Lao-Tzu wrote:

> *Men of the world are clever, self-assured;*
> *I appear stupid and ignorant.*
> *I am on a vast ocean,*
> *Adrift, seemingly aimless.*

This apparent loss is a necessary condition of our return to the true centre from which we have strayed. Only by becoming nothing can we shed the ignorant perversities of our personality. But if in this first initiation into the mystery of the new life we allow ourselves to be overwhelmed by a sense of something so sheer and vast that henceforth all form is unreal and meaningless, we shall have wrongly contracted out of earthly existence and the dual fidelity to earth and heaven which that existence demands of us.

Even great souls have sometimes been led, through an ecstatic response to disembodied spirit, to misconceive the nature of Reality in relation to the manifested world. Particularly in the far East, where the individualistic temper of mind, long established to excess in Western man, is little developed and those strong defences which individualism has built up against the primordial forces of the Absolute are wanting, men have been dazzled by the Infinite into repudiating as altogether illusory the realm of light and shadow in which we move, haltingly and often harmfully, as evolving human beings.

This contempt for relative reality seldom affects the prophetic type, those robustly moral characters of whom Isaiah was a sublime example. When, in the temple, he saw the Lord sitting upon a throne, high and lifted up and surrounded with Seraphims, he exclaimed: "Woe is me! for I am undone; because I am a man of unclean lips; for mine eyes have seen the King, the Lord of Hosts."

But this awesome vision, far from uprooting him from the earth, which the Seraphims declared to be full of the

Lord's glory, culminated in a conviction that his sin was purged and in a renewed readiness to stride forth into the world upon his prophetic and admonitory mission.

There is a world of difference between such apocalyptic occasions, in which the Jewish scriptures abound, and the emotional fervour of a revivalistic meeting. But we know too much today of religious zealots and the fanaticism which they can inspire to take even the most impressive of them on trust. Their zeal may rouse and quicken the dormant spirit, but it can seldom really enlighten. Certainly if the Silence impelled a man forthwith to denounce the iniquities of his fellow-beings, and call them to repentance, it would be regarded by any humble mystic or, for that matter by any experienced psychologist, as of dubious value.

For one of the effects of the Silence, if it has penetrated our souls at all deeply, is to make us sufficiently sensitive to spiritual reality to know that any kind of compulsive action, even if it seems morally laudable in its purpose, is alien to the dimension into which we have been drawn.

Fundamentally what the Silence tells us, when we are capable of hearing its wordless wisdom, is that, in the essence of our Being, the kind of action to which we have hitherto been impelled or by which we have striven to justify our existence, has no place. By temporarily relinquishing such action we are already learning that the Presence with which we have begun to commune, is Itself a stranger to action as we have practised it. Essentially Its only act is to BE, but It so wholly IS that all action is contained in It. Its acts are so divinely right because in Itself It has no need to act. Its nature is to love and Its love finds expression not in action as such, but in creation.

How little conscious we have previously been of this realm of Primal, unconditioned Being in our ordinary existence is shown by the importance we have attached to action for its own sake. We have acted or, rather, reacted to the compulsions of life so incessantly and restlessly because inaction, when we have, in a measure, lapsed into it, has been no more than a temporary lull in which to take breath. Hitherto action and inaction have been for us irreconcilable opposites instead of a single wave which flows and ebbs in the ocean of Being from which we draw our life and strength. If we were truly at home in this ocean, inaction for us would no longer be a denial of action, but a mode of it. And only when they harmoniously combine, is real action possible.

But most of us today are so insecurely related to those unseen depths that the storms and tides or minor currents which fret the surface of life carry us hither and thither and the depth itself has become something in which we fear to be engulfed. When there is nothing in the outer world to distract our mind and senses, we are overcome by a sort of vertigo, a fear of the emptiness in ourselves from which we can only escape into sleep or vacancy.

This fear is behind all our efforts to impose ourselves upon our world and foils our attempts to enter into communion with it. It is because we have lost touch with what we really are that we are driven in every way to strengthen our belief in our separate identity and in our precarious control over life. But the very notion of ourselves as detached individuals and of existence as a private possession is illusory. Existence is total and is only ours in the degree that we share in its totality. Until we realize this, we shall continue to snatch at life in countless ways because we have lost our assurance of belonging to it and know no way of regaining this.

When we have fully acknowledged this, we are ready to enter the Silence of the inner world. The first condition of entering it is that we should reduce and ultimately abandon our interested claims on existence. Our existence has come so much to consist of these claims that in abandoning them we may seem at first to have lost all incentive for life and even our foothold in it. It was by confronting and eventually opposing ourselves to people and things that we became conscious of them and of ourselves as existing independently.

This had to be. But the view of life and of ourselves which we have thus formed is fatally partial. It has inflicted on us a wound which must be healed if we are ever to be spiritually whole. And it can only be healed by beginning consciously to participate in a life which is infinitely more than we are, but in which we, also, are infinitely more than all our efforts to assert ourselves could ever make us.

3

We enter the inner world to discover and develop our sense of this "more". This does not mean that we cannot experience it in our relations with the outer world. But until we are reunited with our own depths, we can only dabble in the shallows of the sea that washes over it or be tossed about in the breakers upon its shore.

We enter the silence of the inner world to recover these depths and to learn that when we abandon our will to assert our own existence, we belong to a Being which affirms us. This, in truth, is what we are when the distracted movement of our vitality and mentality and the incessant flicker of sense-impressions are stilled. Freed from the shadow-play of our false personalities, life ceases to possess the form we have imposed upon it. The deluding light of desire and attachment has gone out, if only at first for precarious moments, and we are in the dark of life's basic anonymity. This can be a painful, even an agonizing experience. At the very moment when we are being resumed in life, we can be conscious only of its absence, of a terrible emptiness and dissolution.

Nearly all the great mystics have spoken, in their own

way, of this dark night of sense or soul or of the tunnel or forest through which the pilgrim has to pass to the new light which at first may be less than a glimmer in the gloom. But this darkness is not as the darkness of the world which masquerades so garishly as light. It is that "dazzling dark" of which Henry Vaughan wrote, which mediates to our spiritual senses the eternal light of the real.

Nevertheless this dark night can only be endured, as it can only be entered, by a sustained act of faith. It may, indeed, seem to be forced upon us through some tragic turn of circumstance or by the inexorable withdrawal from within of the light by which we have hitherto habitually lived. But however it comes to us, we can only make it our own and progress through it by an act of total acceptance. This night and our own emptiness are the same thing and until we are empty of desire and expectation or of regret or resentment, the light within the darkness cannot begin to manifest. Instead of being the womb from which we are to be reborn, the darkness will seem only a tomb in which we are buried alive.

We can hardly escape at times, particularly at our first entrance into this no-man's land of the human spirit, such a negative sensation of the night, as a region vast and void as those infinite spaces which terrified the finite mind of Pascal, a region in which life, if it exists, does so in a dimension and to a degree irreducible to the small humble needs of man. All the intimacies which make human life dear to us, the intimacies of touch and sight, or of voices engaged in that endless dialogue of eye and tongue by which we communicate with each other – all have vanished into this blank void in which we are become lonely cyphers.

And yet there *are* voices to reassure us, the voices of those who have travelled this way before us and proved it to be a gateway to a realm of pure light and immeasurable fullness. They tell us that to enter and sustain ourselves in the Silence we must have love as well as faith. We have come to it not only to escape distraction and the incessant noise of ourselves, but to cast down the burden of our lovelessness. The words of the anonymous author of *The Cloud of Unknowing* have struck home to us: "All men have matter of sorrow: but most specially he feeleth matter of sorrow that knoweth and feeleth that he *is*."

This may seem a hard saying, but not to the man in whom self-consciousness has become an unbearable impediment to health and wholeness of being. The feeling of oneself as separated from one's true source or at least as so precariously related to it, that one can no longer draw confidently on its infinite resources, or return to it for rest and renewal when exhausted by the strain of self-directed activity, is the ultimate of all human sorrow and torment. All pain may be borne so long as we can feel ourselves sustained by That which eternally is. But when the inward sense of this is withdrawn and we pray for the mercy of Its presence apparently in vain, then truly are we forsaken by That which alone gives to life and self its meaning. And since the being of God is the eternal love, in which life finds its creative rhythm and consummation, to feel that we exist outside the pale of this love is to know the full horror of our outcast state.

For a man who thus knows and feels that he *is*, experiences the hell of being utterly alone with the Babel of himself. It is the exact opposite of the condition of a perfect lover, described by the author of *The Cloud of Unknowing*, whose intent is "only and utterly to spoil himself of himself . . . and not admit or suffer to be clothed but only in that thing that he loveth; and that not only for a time, but endlessly to be enwrapped therein in full and final forfeiting of himself."

It is that we may utterly unclothe ourselves of all manner of feeling of self so that we may be clothed "with the gracious feeling of God himself" that we commit ourselves

[129]

5

to the Silence. For when all the vanities of selfhood have fallen off, we fear no longer to be nothing or to be alone, since there can be no greater joy than to be alone with the subject and object of our love and wholly free to give and receive. This, indeed, is heaven, while the aloneness of self is hell. But between the desire thus to unclothe ourselves and any full and final nakedness in a pure love of the Divine there stretches for most of us a long period of probation and purgation in which, often, we may feel lost rather than found and either confuse surrender with defeated resignation or mar it by impatient acts of will.

When we truly live by faith we are supremely willing and utterly unwilful. Instead of asserting ourselves, we acknowledge a power within us of perfect guidance, a power which is as instinct with wisdom and love as with life, which recreates us moment by moment and can work miracles by its grace.

If our surrender is to be more than negative, it is this power which we must continually affirm in faith that we are unfailingly affirmed by it. Thought may lead us to recognize the necessity of such surrender, but to achieve it we have to abandon the security of thought and leap into the unknown and the unthinkable. This something which we have to learn to trust entirely is beyond all the logic that our minds can contrive either to convince ourselves of its presence or to deny it. So long as we cling to such logic to safeguard ourselves against a reality that transcends it, we remain tied to our minds and to the cage in which we have allowed our minds to imprison us. This stultifying security must be totally abandoned before the Silence can begin to open its depths to us.

Denis Saurat has well affirmed this necessity in his book, *The End of Fear*, if his words are rightly understood.

Without suffering and death, one learns nothing. We should not know the difference between the visions of the intellect and the facts.

ENTERING THE SILENCE

*When the intellect intervenes, the idea is finished.
Intelligence consists in halting at the brink of the ditch
one has to jump. Indeed, logically, when one comes to
an empty space, one ought to halt.*
But life is that which leaps.
Intelligence is cowardice.
*The one quality is courage: one attains to truth, as to
life, by courage only. Courage to see all the risk, and
jump.*

The Silence, in one aspect, is this empty space. We
cannot know beforehand what it contains or whether we
shall fall headlong into an abyss. But if and when we
dare the leap of faith, our life will be renewed, through
the death of self-concern, in the greater life from the risk
of which our minds so tenaciously recoiled. We shall
cease to think and know as a defence against the hazard
of unqualified being. We shall return to that indefinable
centre in which we and the eternal "I AM" of Being are
one and in which "the night of thought" is, indeed, as
Coventry Patmore wrote, "the light of perception".

The peace of God, that unassailable calm for which we
all long at heart, is, indeed, beyond understanding. And
the fact that primarily it is our heart which longs for it
indicates where our starting-point must be when we set
out on the journey, long or short, which will lead us to it.
Our task is one of concentration and there are various
centres in our being in which it is possible to concentrate
our consciousness. The Silence embraces them all and
upon each one of them it can shed its benediction. But
the centre in which we need first to invoke and receive
the Silence is the heart, because in the hidden depths of
the heart lie the creative roots of our being and the divine
flame in which we need to be purified and reborn.

This heart which in the Silence will begin to open as we
concentrate our attention on it and, free from all distraction,

pray only to enter into it, is not the physical heart, though that is, as it were, a valve of it. It is the eternal heart of life itself, the sun in that inward heaven which we are here to realize. The pure in heart are those in whom no clouds obscure this central sun and whose natures have been purged of all dross by its undying fire.

This is the heart, centred within us, which we need to enter in the Silence. For until we have found our way into it and begun to yield ourselves to the depths of its power and its peace, no transformation of our life or consciousness can occur, however strenuous our efforts may be to become other than we are. Here, hidden within our breast, "smaller than the smallest atom, greater than the greatest spaces", as the *Katha Upanishad* declares, is the root and the flower of our real being. Here is our divine source and our divine end, our timeless essence and the dynamic will which sustains us in time and inspires us with the urge and the power for creative transformation.

The divine is indescribable as it is unthinkable in its essence. And the new life can only begin when we have abandoned all attempts to reduce it to the measure of our human capacities or make it conform to our own will. We have simply to plunge into it, to be embraced by it as the naked bather by the ocean into which he dives. So long as we hesitate and allow our minds to debate the pros and the cons, we shall remain as we are. Such debate and a growing recognition of our own unreality and insufficiency, may well have preceded the moment of self-committal. But when that moment has come, it must, if it is going to be effective, initiate as total an act of self-giving as we can compass. All creation, on whatever level, involves such an act. It is only the beginning and needs much preparation. But without it no newly centred life can originate.

Admittedly the moment to take the plunge cannot come, however desperate the situation in which we find ourselves, until we have had some intimation of the reality to which we need to surrender. And by intimation I mean something more immediate than a conviction that it is reasonable to assume the existence of such a reality. It is possible to argue as an idealist that a divine idea underlies and informs both ourselves and the material universe without ever experiencing the divine. Our minds are adept at the game of arguing for or against such a conception. And the more we argue, the further we are from the experience which stills and renders unnecessary all argument.

Even a fleeting glimpse of trans-personal reality, a sense, momentary but direct, of the divine Presence, can be enough to awaken in us a longing to adventure into a new dimension of experience, in which we shall surely come nearer to the truth of our being and of all being. For in such glimpses the soul is quickened and it is to deepen and enlarge the knowledge of the soul that we abandon the restless activity of the mind and plunge into the silent ocean of the divine.

In many of us mental habits are so fixed that nothing but the Silence itself, when we have opened a way for it and learnt to keep it open, can dissolve them and gradually complete the surrender which we can only long at heart to be total and entire. But at least we are prevented from assuming that it is entire when in fact much in our nature is still but partially committed. Yet in intention at least there must be an initial act of total surrender, if the new rhythm which will change our life and deliver us from the conflict and confusion of a self-centred existence is to be set in motion.

And if we steadily persist in a positive readiness to receive the peace which passes understanding and to affirm what we receive, our faith will eventually be fulfilled in knowledge. We shall know that we do not call for help in vain, that to every sincere disinterested appeal the unseen power unfailingly responds, though it be in a hidden way. A new awareness of belonging to the whole scheme of things, an awareness rooted in the ultimate mystery of consciousness and life, as a flower or tree are rooted in the darkness of the soil, begins to make itself felt. We divine what in the stress of our former life we had forgotten, that infinitely beyond our own puny self-assertion, we ARE.

Previously, if we had asked ourselves "What am I?" we could only have answered from the circumference of being, "I am legion" or "I am the moods which possess me" or "I am an impotent rebel against another's will or my own cruel fate". Now, when we are ready to answer "I am, or I would be, nothing", we hear, as if in a whisper from a centre of being in which our heart has learnt to rest, "That which I eternally AM, you are". In the heart of the Silence there is a presence, mysterious, all-embracing, re-creative.

This Being which we begin to divine as affirming Itself in us has no form to which we can cling. To experience It we have had to abandon any mental conceptions we may have had of an Almighty, whether religious or philosophical. It is an "I" which cannot be thought. Yet we cannot doubt that it is supremely real. In the boundless depths of our being It lives, the blissful source of all the happiness at which we have selfishly and sorrowfully grasped. It does not seize upon us, as the vital impulses in an unregenerate nature do, compelling us to indulge one part of our being to the exclusion or at the expense of another, but It draws us, calmly and irresistibly, into the embrace of Its wholeness.

What the Silence eventually unveils to us baffles the mind. Yet, as the great teachers declare, "when That is known, all is known". Not the all of discursive knowledge, for such knowledge is endlessly incomplete, but the all of creative insight.

In the dark void which has received us we have a growing sense of revealing light and love that dispels the

ancient creature fear of the primordial force which creates
and destroys all the forms of life. Though awe remains, it
is an awe in which there is no dread either of life or death.
For we have touched a depth in ourselves in which dying
and living are equally blessed modes of union with the
true source and centre of our being. By ceasing to cling to
any form we have renewed our relationship with the
originating genius of all forms.

This experience of the heart of the Silence changes
radically our experience of the world about us. We had
reason previously to regard the phenomenal world as
illusory, though few who are engrossed in it do. For so
long as we had selfish designs upon it we could see it
only partially and, so seen, it was as illusory as the self
which sought to possess and exploit it. But now, as we
grow closer to the ineffable heart of the cosmos and allow
our own heart to beat to its tranquil, yet infinitely potent,
rhythm, we begin to see a world instinct with meaning
and harmony.

Just as when as children we were learning to read, there
came a moment when the separate letters combined to
give a word and a whole world of meaning and com-
munication opened before us, so now what was fragmentary and unrelated or apparently discordant becomes
part of the eternal Word which informs it.

Until we have discovered Silence and what it enshrines,
we cannot thus experience the deep relatedness of everything in life. Silence is the inner space which our faculties
need if they are to function properly. One's words should
be set in Silence as objects are set in space. The forms of
things are inseparable from the space around them and the
more worthy of appreciation they are, the more space
they need in which to reveal themselves. In a crowded
world objects lose their significance or we lose our capacity for seeing it. It is the same with our minds. When
they are congested with anxious or superficial thoughts,

they are lost to truth. We multiply words without meaning.

For until we have learnt to listen silently, we speak without real knowledge and hear without understanding. Fastening upon the words we miss the meaning that flows through them from behind and beyond. For behind every word is an idea which no word can ever make wholly explicit. Ideas descend from a world without form or of far more subtle and fluent form than that which our sensebound mind imposes on our vision. Words are not necessarily impervious to this world. Indeed the aim of every true poet is to capture in language something of its infused harmony and radiance.

But poets are few and even when words are not debased or deformed they commonly serve the lower and opaque levels of the mind or are used as ammunition in a private war between individual interests and attitudes. This is true even of the language used by the learned. It is equally true of our everyday verbal intercourse. How seldom do we understand each other despite all the words we barter. Yet it is well known that those who are well attuned can often communicate without words or merely by verbal hints because they are near to each other in the silence of the mind.

This silence of the mind makes possible a new relationship of immediate perception. We discover that beneath the external surface of the mind is a realm of consciousness which contains our individual minds and unites them. Here, in this wordless region of immediate awareness, we are not shut off from each other by our own private mental world, with its interests and prejudices. Mind here is as vast, all inclusive and penetrating as space, and every expression of thought springs from this unexpressed source. When we are in union with it, we are in union with the essence of every other mind, however it may differ in its mental habits or outlook.

This silent region of the mind is, also, a silence of the heart. For in the deeper and higher consciousness heart and mind are undivided. When we are in rapport with it we understand by sympathy and identification. This does not prevent us from perceiving error or confusion where they exist in someone's reasoning. But we see beneath these the truth that is struggling to find utterance, and where the expression is inadequate, we yet grasp the meaning. For we are in touch with what is unexpressed in the speaker's mind as it is in our own.

This, of course, applies equally to any book, with deep meaning in it, which we wish to understand. We shall never receive the meaning of such books unless we read them with a silent, receptive mind instead of grasping at the words externally. We have to allow ourselves to sink into that wordless region within us in which meaning originates and then let the words rise again to the surface of our consciousness, charged with the truth which they drew from that region in the creative mind which we share with their author. This is particularly necessary when we are reading any scriptures or great poetry. But all true intercourse with others depends on this mutual communion with the Silence which underlies all speech.

To discover the Silence, then, in solitary meditation is to establish a relationship with our creative source which transforms our relations with the whole of objective existence, with the natural world and our fellow-beings. In it we are weaned from that attachment to ourselves and to the phenomenal world which prevents us from living imaginatively.

This weaning is, of course, accomplished in us in other ways than in the stillness and emptiness of solitary meditation. For the way to reality is in every situation which encourages or compels us to commit ourselves to life more fundamentally. It offers itself to us in the testings of personal tragedy or frustration, in times when we can only

5*

patiently suffer and endure, and in the opportunities of devoted service or of dedication to a work which demands all we have to give in courage, insight and skill. Indeed there is no situation, however apparently discouraging or unbearable or however joyous and uplifting, in which we cannot learn to participate in life more deeply, to respond more finely to the spirit's hidden directives, to love more sensitively and relate ourselves more intelligently to the genius of truth in all that is.

But without prayerful contemplation we cannot come really near to the heart of life, still less maintain our nearness, though such contemplation may take many forms. All of them to be valid must help to draw us into a dimension of experience in which we are divested of the self which we had supposed ourselves to be.

In this return to our origin we have regained the starting-point from which man began his journey into consciousness and first found himself as an individual. Pre-historic man, as I have said, awoke at some point in his evolution from a state of sleep-walking, in which he moved darkly with the stream of life and obedient to the direction of cosmic mind, into awareness of a world separate from himself and of himself as separate from the world. Previously he was only the field in which divine and natural forces commingled, as in the Group-Soul. He had yet to think individually. Only when he began to perceive an object as relatively detached from himself, did he become a distinctively human being in other than a biological sense. Later he enlarged his new perception by naming objects, and the world which the human mind was to order and classify in elaborate detail took shape.

Yet though the objects, seen and named, multiplied as man's mind extended its range and reach, they were for long not seen in isolation. Separate as each was in his sensory grasp, they were felt to be related through a Something within, which was common to them all. And it was this Something within, as I have shown, which invested them for primitive man with a sacredness that must not be desecrated.

Yet eventually it *was* desecrated, because man himself fell into disunity in his greedy pursuit of multiplicity. He identified himself with his body and exploited the body of life. Hence the necessity of a return, the need "to travel back and tread again that ancient track".

But the return is, also, a going forward into a new condition, of which man has only begun to realize the need and the possibility. For we return with a consciousness which can never again relapse into the world of mindless sensation in which the sleep-walker lived. In entering the Silence, in submitting to become nothing, we may seem to die to the world of forms and names and to live only in That which transcends them. But the faculties of discrimination and analysis which we have inherited from countless generations of thinking, watchful and measuring men are only in temporary abeyance. In the Void to which we have surrendered they are being re-conditioned in their creative source. Thus resumed in Being, they cease to be instruments of a critical enmity against life and become instead organs of vision by means of which we perceive from within the distinctive forms in which the divine Spirit images some aspect of its formless essence.

These forms are legion. They are all about us. We cannot lift our eyes but the creative Spirit is there taking shape and revealing in that shape some part, however minute, of Its great design. It may even be, as Tennyson declared, that if we could understand the little flower in the crannied wall, what it is "root and all, and all in all", we should know "what God and man is". But it is preeminently in and through man that the creative spirit can reveal Its inner nature. It is in and through our consciousness, when the doors of perception are cleansed, that the Supreme Knower makes Himself known.

The deeper, therefore, we enter through the Silence into communion with the divine, the more will our faith flower in knowledge. The Silence will begin to speak. Light will shine in the darkness into which the divided self has died, and the soul, upon which that self had imposed its contractive will, will be free at last to open to that "Spirit of golden radiance" which is its true lover and to conceive and bring to birth the new man, the child of grace and understanding.

❁

CHAPTER SEVEN

Love Set Free

1

That Something to which we have drawn nearer in the
Silence begins to reveal its innermost nature in what we
can, perhaps, best describe as a growing aura of love and
light. During our life we have all felt something of the
magic of love as directly as we have felt the rays of the
sun. But by deepening our experience of what love is
when undistorted by any hunger for possession, we draw
nearer to an understanding of the creative mystery of
which love is the root and the flower.

"All the world is secretly maddened by the mystery of
love," wrote Coventry Patmore, "and continually seeks its
solution everywhere but where it is to be found." Lovers,
in the first rapture of mutual recognition, come near to
love's mystery when they live it without teasing questions
and are still too "translated", to borrow Bottom's word, to
sensationalize it. But that first moment of imaginative
gratitude for the pure presence of another – a gift sufficient
in itself to satisfy the soul, but not the body, inevitably
passes.

> *Love's mysteries in souls do grow,*
> *But yet the body is the book.*

And, too often, both the ecstasy and the mystery of love are
dissipated in the thumbed pages of that book.

Love should enlighten, should quicken, in an ever
deeper degree, grace and vision. But in the fire and smoke

of the body's desires its light is dimmed or quenched. It is by fidelity to the light within it that love grows and is true to its genius. For the union of love and light is also the union of life and truth. In their essence love and light are inseparable. When they fall apart, each ceases to be itself. For they are dual modes of the one creative and creating mystery.

But considered in their dual aspect love is feminine; the light which informs it is masculine. Through love we feel. The light, shining through our intelligence, clarifies love's feeling and is itself warmed and vitally blessed by it. We are born into this world with the instinct for love which begot us, though our expression of that instinct is at first so elementary as to be all need and demand. But even then, as we suck blindly at the breasts of mothering life, the light shines uncomprehended in the darkness of instinct. And as it directs us on the path of our growth from infancy to childhood and from childhood to manhood, its rays increasingly stimulate the mind to independent thought and action. But, more often than not, this action, through false direction, is pursued as an end in itself or in the service of our selfish interests.

In this way we betray the heart, which, deprived of its guiding light, itself falls into excess, feeding on what the senses offer or on sentimentality, vague raptures and private despairs. It is thus that we all, in different degrees, have fallen out of the divine order, in which love and light are united in a perfect marriage of consciousness and life.

Because, in the goodness of the creative will, truth and love blend perfectly together, we cannot offend against one of them without violating the other. If we offend against love, what we take in pride of mind for incisive truth reflects only the designs we have upon life, our bias against it or the wants we need to satisfy. And if we disregard the justice of truth, no passionate protestations of love can save us from eventual disillusionment. We cannot experience truth until we are wholly submissive to it. Then the light which shines with increasing purity through the higher faculties of the mind will descend into the heart and make its home there, consecrated and humanized by love.

In the Void which has opened within us in the Silence, we begin to be conscious of this descent, through which the quality both of our feeling and our thought is changed, as they interpenetrate and interfuse with each other. We become aware of the intermingling of love and light in the invisible centre of our being and from this springs a new and expanded feeling of what we are. We have spoken of the sense of peace as the first-fruit of the Silence, a peace which is other than an absence of noise or a negative quiet. So it is when a love, devoid of desire and longing, awakens in our hearts and enfolds us in the embrace of its mystery.

The vital instinct of love, as previously we had known it, may seem to have died in a night of non-feeling. But what is born of this death is a love which is transparent to the light and which enables the evolving soul to enter into ever deeper and more intimate union with the spirit, and so to feel and know in a single, undivided act. We are laid asleep in body as an infant in his mother's arms. But in spirit we are awake and the Mother to whom we have yielded our will is no longer that primal Mother whose body is the natural world and who with equal lust conceives, nourishes and devours the children of her womb. This Great Mother of primitive myth and ritual denies to her children the individual consciousness which threatens her sovereignty. Her love is possession and is indistinguishable from the blind instinct of life.

It is, doubtless, for this reason that in so many historical religions God is imaged as exclusively male and the feminine principle relegated to the realm of fallen Nature. But the divine Nature, which embraces the natural life that It infinitely surpasses, is not fallen. And in It the feminine principle is as creatively pure as the male. To be re-born of the spirit we require a Mother as well as a Father, as we did at our first birth into the body. But the unseen parents of our new being are of equal status. They are united in the divine Nature of which love is the feminine principle and light the masculine.

When in the Silence we begin to feel the approach of this divine Mother of our being as love, we are not overwhelmed by her power as expressed in the passion of the flesh, but are conscious of a soft suffusion of light, a radiance of relationship, in the darkness of her presence. For her love, unlike that of our primal Mother, Eve, is also wisdom. She is "Sancta Sophia" – tranquil, serene, compassionate, forgiving. In her the instincts of natural life are transformed into insights, its lusts into the healing and regenerative power of charity.

This is the true Mother of our soul, as Eve was the mother of our body, and in and through her our soul opens to receive the divine spirit and become a home for it in and beyond the world of time and change, so that it may mould us more and more closely in the likeness of its eternal Self.

It is thus that by offering ourselves to the mystery within our hearts the tension and anxieties induced by our bondage to temporal circumstance are relaxed and the ground is prepared in which a consciousness of what we truly are will grow. The ground is prepared in the Silence, but it must be kept free of weeds, if this new consciousness is not to be choked at birth. The seeds of such weeds, borne on the winds of life or carried by our fellow creatures, will continue to take root in our emotional nature for as long as we make them our own – seeds of envy and enmity, sensuality and pride, anger or resentment, vanity and acquisitiveness.

If we try to suppress such feelings, they merely root

[144]

themselves more deeply. But if we make and maintain a habit of observing them attentively, we realize before long that they are as foreign to what we really are as the rash of an infectious disease. As a result they have less and less power to take us unaware and love is increasingly free to work unimpeded in our hearts and minds, kindling the light of spiritual understanding and transforming what before was abstract knowledge into living truth. And the more conscious we become of love's healing power, present in the heart of things and serenely flowing from its secret depths into our souls, the more surely are we reconciled with life and drawn into harmony with its infinite meaning and goodness.

The hostility of man to life, displayed at its crudest today in the declared intention of some of our technocrats to "conquer the universe", is, in fact, a pathetic confession of inward defeat. Generally, however, distrust of life with consequent anxiety manifests in unrest or apathy and impels men to resort to physical intoxication both to heighten and relax the tension. Hence the ubiquitous appeal of alcohol and sex and also the unconfessed attractiveness of war as a desperate means of exploding frustration. Indeed those who hear at their back "Time's winged chariot hurrying near" and can see ahead only "*deserts* of vast eternity", as if eternity were an everlasting emptiness instead of an ever-present fullness, have every reason to heighten the sensation of existence by tearing their "pleasures with rough strife Through the iron gates of life".

In them, as in all of us until we are restored to our true nature in which the earthly in us is redeemed by what is heavenly, there is a feud between time and eternity, between that superficial and transient time measured by our senses and that deep duration in which past, present and future meet in an eternal "now". To this feud we owe all our unrest, since time unanchored in the whole and constant is forever hurrying us on to goals that can never be reached, while an eternity conceived by the mind as divorced from time or unrelated to it, is, indeed, a "desert" of infinite abstraction.

But in the love which the Silence imperceptibly discloses to our hearts, as in the peace which precedes and accompanies it, the apparent gulf which we have allowed to open between timeless being and temporal becoming begins to close, and our distrust of life, which is the converse of our fear of death, dissolves in a direct experience of That Which has neither beginning nor end and of Which all things, as they manifest, are meant to be a unique expression.

To become conscious of our reality as spiritual beings does not withdraw us from earthly existence or the realm of time. But we become aware that we belong to an order of being to which existence in time owes all the relative reality it possesses and without which it possesses no reality at all. Our earthly substance and human faculties are the medium in which the Spirit works, but with the freedom of an artist in no way bound to the particular medium in and through which he creates. A true artist studies the nature and the needs of his medium, and his creative freedom will be enhanced by the apparent limitation which his medium imposes. But his genius transcends all the forms to which it gives itself in the act of imagining them and is wholly original. Even so the spirit transcends each and every exercise of its creative faculty, and its eternal quality, its wholeness as containing all possibilities of expression, is in no way affected, still less diminished, by the fact that it is in love, as William Blake wrote, "with the productions of time".

This truth is expressed by Krishna in the *Bhagavad-Gita* when, speaking as the Divine Spirit incarnate, he says:

Consider me: I am not bound by any sort of duty. There is nothing which I do not already possess; nothing I have yet to acquire. But I go on working, nevertheless. . . . If I were to stop, mankind would be lost.

He is speaking here in his aspect as Creator. But in his essence, as he says elsewhere, "I am unborn, my Self is changeless. Though I seem to be born, it is only seeming." This unborn and undying essence we begin, however faintly at first, to realize as the Silence within and our receptiveness to it deepens. And this realization is the root of the peace and the love which take possession of us and of the sense we have that in renouncing the life we had tried to possess, we receive it again as a free gift and in incomparably fuller measure. So long as love in us is engrossed in a desire for life which turns outward to assuage its hunger or discharge its force, we cannot know any lasting peace. For, in truth, it is not things we desire, but eternity, as Nietzsche said, a deep, deep eternity. In our most sensual as in our most ideal cravings this is the satisfaction for which we unconsciously or consciously long. But eternity has no form that can be possessed. It only can inform us when, amid the forms of life, we abandon all desire to possess any of them. In this way we find, within, the primordial source from which both love and life spring and in which they are at one with the light of a consciousness that no darkness can quench.

By going into the solitude of our souls and emptying them of all the recurrent thoughts, feelings and desires which we have built into a false image of ourselves, we thus make it possible to enter into a new and real relationship with the powers within us and the world around us, whose diverse forms image some aspect of the same infinite being which expresses itself in us. For in that emptiness of self our soul is delivered from the bondage which life and our self-concern have imposed upon it, all that burden of anxious anticipation or regret which have prevented the soul from realizing its true nature and opening to the light of the Spirit.

Many people use the words soul and spirit indiscriminately, as if they meant the same thing. But as the Greeks were careful to show, they represent two distinct, though intimately related, principles of all sentient being. Spirit, as I have said, while omni-present, is timeless and, as pure will and consciousness, is not subject to growth or change. But the soul in each of us grows as we grow. It is both what we are and what we may become. It takes its form from the stage in life which we have reached and the level of our nature on which we are living. For the soul is essentially receptive. All our experience sinks deep into its plastic substance and takes there the shape given to it by the mind.

When, in childhood and youth, we are immersed in the body and in natural life, our soul reflects our relationship to that level of our being. If it is a pure relationship, untainted by selfish appetite, our soul is in union with the great soul of nature and partakes of its beauty and vitality. But except in early childhood we are never purely attached to nature, but to all the feelings and thoughts, the aspirations and desires, which increasingly constitute what we personally are.

This is the life within us of which our soul becomes the image. And if that life is turbulent or mean, if our thoughts are false and what we pursue as good is evil, our soul is marred and its potential beauty obscured. Potentially the soul is beautiful. For it is the cup which, at every level of our growth, can be filled with the eternal wine of the spirit. That is the creative intention of life. But for it to be fulfilled we have not only to purify our thoughts and impulses, so that the cup may be cleansed to receive the sacramental wine. We have, also, to rise above the outlook associated with the external and sensory level of our being to a higher and interior level on which we discover a new order both of Truth and Goodness.

Analysts have drawn a distinction between our animal

LOVE SET FREE

and our human soul. In this view our animal soul is the psychic counterpart of our earthly nature and, as such, subject to the lusts of the body, its rapacity, sloth and ignorance, though gifted with a wonderful intelligence of its own. Our human soul, on the other hand, is the image, still incomplete, of the inward arche-typal Self with which it aspires to unite and the qualities of which it reflects in all the finer characteristics and impulses of the distinctively human person.

Yet these two souls, linked respectively with the sub-human and the super-human levels of our being are but the outer and the inner spheres of the One Soul which embraces every level of our nature and unites us with the universal Soul of life. This is the soul through which we evolve as we ascend from one level of our nature to another. As we grow in intelligence and sensibility, our animal nature is civilized, and through spiritual aspiration and concentration our human personality is brought ever nearer to completion in its divine prototype.

This ascent does not involve a denial of the sensory level of our being, but it does eventually involve a total subordination of that level to the direction of spiritual perception and its values.

By this inward ascent our soul, realizing its original beauty, becomes the true mediator in us between heaven, the spiritual world, and earth, the world of nature, and so the channel through which the body is spiritually redeemed. It is then the organ through which the creative and regenerating energy of love flows.

This is the love, at once transcending and fulfilling self-love, that we begin to experience. If there were no soul ready to receive the enlightening spirit, there would be no love in our hearts and without such love the naked light of spirit would consume us. We get a faint impression of what such un-souled light would be in the thought of those who pursue truth without mercy or compassion and are ready to destroy a world for a system of ideas.

Those, too, who exploit the natural world mechanically, offend against the soul of nature. In the words of a Chinese sage, "they do not use their hearts in the enjoyment of outward things, but use outward things as a means of delighting their hearts." It is through the soul that the Spirit, as pure consciousness, descends into sensitive nature which needs to receive and be enlightened by it. In this marriage of spirit and soul the old hostility, overt or furtive, between sense and intelligence in man is resolved.

So long as the soul is tied to the body's appetites there can be no true marriage with the spirit and our natural feelings and affections will, after a certain point, hinder our growth, because they will attach us to the transient. This is the meaning of the myths and legends which figure the rescue of the maiden from the dragon. The spirit liberates the soul by enlightening it, but the soul humanizes the spirit by loving it and together they create the whole man who, in his wisdom, knows and lives the truth and rejoices in its goodness.

By this union of spirit and soul the division between heart and mind is healed. The tree of Knowledge is only fruitful when it is, also, the tree of Life and this living knowledge is born of the love that conjoins the changeless inner Self which is our spirit with our evolving soul. Our soul, for long submerged in the darkness of primal nature, grows through human experience into ever closer relationship with the informing light of that true Self. But imperfectly souled spirit in man, manifesting as rootless rationality, is as self-destructive as the feverish cravings of an un-illumined Psyche.

When, however, in the void of the Silence we fully realize that, as puppets of life, however bustling or consequential, we are nothing and that the self we have been struggling to preserve and gratify is only a series of conditioned reflexes, we can begin to live, not in reaction to external life, but as an act of being. In such being the self-will which distorts the spirit's awareness in the ruthless idealism of the mind or seduces the soul through the senses dissolves. The freed soul opens to the light which shines in its own central depths and love is re-conceived and re-born, a love released from its bonds and so joyous in its total affirmation of Being that there is no room in it for either self-love or self-hate. To love thus is not to deny what Henry James called "the sacred fount" of life or its sacred flame. Rather it is to bathe in the one and burn in the other with a pure passion in which light and darkness meet in rapt communion.

2

When the liberated soul is thus united with the spirit, the body is also truly at rest in its own kingdom. The tensions and excitements to which we constantly subject it pervert the rhythm of its unconscious life. In that unconscious life the spirit is present as it is in deep sleep, renewing and sustaining our strength. But in the self-conscious life in which we have largely lost the ability to live and love beyond ourselves, we exist in the shallows of our being, out of contact with either the depths or the heights in which the invisible power of the spirit resides. Consequently we are impoverished and become sick in body and mind and the cry goes up, "You *must* relax", which is a contradiction in terms. For "must" implies an act of self-will which is itself the cause of all wasteful tension.

True relaxation is an act of faith and of love directed attentively to any tautened part of the body or mind. Simply to become fully aware in this way of points or areas of tension is to relax them. By such acts of applied recollection and inward attention we begin to realize our identity with the spirit which is unattached to the body that it informs. The more we love in and by the grace of this spirit, the less do we perversely cling to the body and thwart the healing inflow of life. The more alight and alive we are in soul, the more relaxed we are in body. For in our released souls we know that we belong to eternal life and so have no need for self-preservation. Realizing that neither life nor death can separate us from the Love which is the very principle of our being and the Life to which we so wholly belong, we need no longer cling to our bodies as if we existed only in them.

Our physical body is not, as materialists suggest, a mere chemical compound. It is a condensation of the soul, which is at first almost wholly immersed in the body, but gradually emerges as the feeling organ of consciousness. For a time we feel through the physical senses only and our consciousness is confined within their range. But while the soul interpenetrates the physical body and may seem at first to be no more than a sensitive adjunct of it, it has a body of its own which extends beyond the physical and vital sheaths of our being. And this soul body, through its quicker vibration, is responsive to a super-sensuous realm.

It is through possession of this body that, as we evolve, we become conscious in our souls of a spiritual world. This would not be possible, did we not, also, possess an independent spiritual body, an intelligible form, which penetrates and illuminates both our psychic and our physical bodies without being tied to either. Our soul, therefore, the faculty through which we feel, is linked with natural life, through its relation with the physical body, and with a super-physical life through its union with the spiritual body. And as its responsiveness to the unseen world of the spirit grows stronger, it becomes increasingly conscious of the unity manifesting through all forms of life and of the Supreme Being and Consciousness in which all living creatures subsist and which is immeasurably within and beyond each one of them.

This is the source of the new awareness, a faculty of direct perception and cognition independent of the physical senses, to which our soul begins to awake in the Silence, as we cease to cling to our bodies or to identify ourselves with the picture of the world which we receive through them or with the transient moods and thoughts excited by external events. It is equally the source of the compassionate love which begins to heal the conflict in our hearts, because the channels through which it flows and which we have blocked by our addiction to mental strife and physical sensation, have been allowed to open. Now, all the senses which we have misused can become channels of spirit, as William Blake called them. What we experience through them is no longer the pleasure-pain of a desire which divides, but the bliss and benediction of a love which, even in suffering, unites with the whole of life.

Thus the change of consciousness which transforms and renews us springs from and brings with it a sense of belonging to a life infinitely greater than our own, of which we feel, with increasing intimacy, that we are inseparably a part. Consciousness means literally "knowing-together". Until heart, mind and body are thus gathered together and obedient to a higher principle, our knowledge, however extensive it may be, is fragmentary and external. Its contents are imperfectly co-ordinated, if not contradictory. The sensory world and what our minds deduce from it, the inner worlds of our dreams and aspirations, of our baffled feelings or innate ideas fail, except in rare moments, to agree. They cannot form a whole because we have yet to find the centre, within and beyond ourselves, in which they unite.

Faith alone enables us to surrender to the power of the

Living Spirit which rewards and justifies our faith. In our purest moments of release from self-concern in the past we have had intimations of this treasure of abundant life and wholeness which was ours to receive. We have touched momentarily a condition in which everything had a heightened significance, moments, it may be, of intense æsthetic enjoyment or even of mystical communion with that unearthly Presence who

> *comes with western winds, with evening's*
> *wandering airs,*
> *With that clear dusk of heaven that brings the*
> *thickest stars.*

In such moments our capacity to live beyond ourselves has been stretched far enough to make us poignantly conscious of the narrow poverty of our ordinary existence. Yet through fear of the unknown dimensions beyond our sensory shell or through a still strong attachment to its material comforts we have failed to build anything on such moments, failed to set ourselves to the task of becoming what they showed us we might be and veritably are.

But now, if we persist in allowing the divine seed of light hidden within us to become the growing point of a new Self, that inner realm, which previously was as evanescent as a dream, will begin to infuse reality into all we see and do. Our soul is native to that world and as it extends its power over the outer personality, we begin to see people and things from within and to feel ourselves united with them through what is immortal in our nature and in theirs. We begin, in Clare Cameron's words, "to hear the music of the spirit in all things – not only in the wind, bird-song, sea, the seasons, but in the cadences of human voices, struggling through flesh to express the feelings of the soul, in the movement of human hands as well as the fire on the hearth, in all that man strives to create through the power within him, however much in his ignorance he may mistranslate or distort."*

This is the ultimate gift of love, the gift of organic union, which manifests on every level of life from the fusion of male and female cells to the union of the soul with its Creator. Self-consciousness, in the separative sense of the word, is the enemy of such union. Yet, in a deeper sense, it is its condition and fulfilment. For without self-knowledge we cannot know another nor can the sense of identity, necessary to relationship, be established. Love enlarges that sense until it unites us with the whole of ourselves and of life. For to love someone is to be really conscious of him or her. And we can only be thus conscious of other persons by knowing them in ourself and knowing ourself in them. It is by thus making room for another person, without blame or judgement, with all his likeable or, to us, unlikeable qualities, which exist in some degree in ourselves, that a mutually creative relationship becomes possible.

The seat of real consciousness is the inner Soul or Self, to which all the senses are meant to minister. But the self-consciousness which disables and divides clings to the outer world or recoils from it. This outer world is always fluctuating and if we experience it only from the surface of our being, we are adrift on a perilous sea and all our struggles to find meaning in it and in ourselves will be ineffectual. The feeling that we are at the mercy of un-predictable changes and hazards, even in people to whom we are attached and upon whom we depend, makes us calculating. We have to defend ourselves, if possible, against the treachery of circumstance. And this may lead some even to try to buy the affection or the emotional security which they so desperately need to solace their loneliness. The ultimate treachery, in such a view, is death and against it there is no defence. Either we must

* In *Science of Thought Review*, May 1962.

accept it and so learn to die the death which gives new meaning to life, or go on struggling to preserve our existence for as long as possible against the certainty of extinction.

For there is no doubt that the self to which most of us cling and which we identify with the body will be extinguished, though not necessarily at once, by physical death. Hell and purgatory or some gentler school of illumination may await it after that. But life tolerates division only so long as it serves a creative purpose. We are meant to grow through the self-consciousness which divides and curtails into that fullness of being and knowing in which we surrender all the partial knowledge we have painfully acquired to that greater Self in whom real consciousness resides. The illusion of separateness was necessary to make that possible.

Then only can we truly be said to love. Admittedly without the power of love within us, however diminished, we could not live at all. For life itself is an emanation of love. Acute self-consciousness is obviously fatal to the realization of that union in difference in which love is fulfilled. But even in its subtler manifestations, as in a sensibility too easily wounded or a mind too active to receive in depth, it can thwart that unguarded interchange of being which love inspires. But all the hindrances to love which self-consciousness imposes upon the fearless flow of the Spirit disappear when we are humble enough to see that we have no love of our own to give, that what we give is given to us by the unseen Power which creates and sustains us, and that the range and quality of our giving depend wholly on our receptive attunement.

We could not love or be loved by another, were it not for this unseen Power which is present in us both and between and around us, the Power which, in Dante's vision, binds together all the scattered leaves of the universe by the inspiration of Its wholeness and which can draw all opposites into a union of magnetic accord. In a work of art the artist and the human being meet in something higher. And all the art of love in which we blend with the person or the object that we contemplate, giving and receiving together the infinite breath of life entrusted to us, is made possible by this "something higher", this unseen third in the dialogue of human encounter, which unites everywhere the two in meaningful relationship.

Thus it is that in such love we begin to experience life and death, the ultimate two, as one. For we are all secretly in love with death though it is only in our moments of intensest life that we fully declare our love. Lovers die to live in each other and find their utmost felicity in so doing. This, indeed, is not only the condition of highest bliss, but the law which governs the perpetuation of life on all levels. But except in ecstatic moments the impulse of self-preservation dominant in the body prevails generally over that of self-giving or at least the two impulses are in uneasy counterpoise.

This is bound to be until we are at home in the inner life of the soul. For the soul, though intimately in touch with the sensible world and for long immersed in it, has its origin in the ideal world, the world of spirit, and so is not subject to the tyranny of time. It is the organizing principle in man. On whatever level of his being it is most active, it creates a whole, healing division and endowing with beauty the body which it informs. In its descent from its spiritual home into the world of physical manifestation it becomes increasingly involved in denser degrees of matter. The four elements of etheric fire, of air, water and earth traditionally represent the four planes of being through which it passes in dreamlike trance on its journey into earthly incarnation.

In returning to its spiritual source it retraces its steps with increasing awareness as it rises through the physical plane of unconscious instinct and the water of sensuous or passional feeling, into the lucid air of thought, and ultimately, when purified of all attachment, reunites with the radiant Light which begot it and which it intuitively reflects.

In most people this ascent of the soul through progressively finer planes of experience is only tentative during their life-time and waits to be continued and completed until death frees the soul from its densest earthly sheath. But in all of us the four planes exist as psychological grades or aspects of being and each of us tends to be more active or reflective on one or other of them according as one element predominates in our disposition. Indeed human types, whether earthly or spiritual, emotional or intellectual, can be classified on these lines. But only as the soul draws nearer to its spiritual source and awakens from the sleep of natural life can it fulfil its vocation as the integrator of our consciousness on all its levels and the harmonizer of the four elements of which our being is composed.

Thus, as life in the soul becomes real to us and we participate in it more and more, we become increasingly sure that as souls we outlive the life of the body. Such knowledge will not come to us by taking thought for thought's sake. It has to be lived to be known and for this we need the humility to abandon all negative questioning so that the new meaning, which the soul possesses through its union with the world of spirit, may inform and animate our lives. The more intimately it does so, the more will it be found to accord with the deeper reason of our being. In the light of that deeper reason all the anxious attachment to physical life and its mental concerns which restricts both love and vision will be seen to be unreal and irrelevant.

Thus in the silence of our souls love and light grow in power together and as they infuse their reality into our will, as well as into our senses and intelligence, and we become more finely responsive to their interplay, heart and mind reunite. By some mysterious alchemy the feeling, by which we participate in life, and the thought, by which we can detach ourselves from it as critical onlookers, cease to be divided. No longer need we fear to feel lest we should be carried away by feeling into excesses which a cool judgement would deplore. Nor, on the other hand, will the intellect, in the pride of its analytical powers, destroy the life which it so cleverly dissects.

For the seemingly inescapable conflict between heart and mind, through which self-consciousness develops, is not final. It characterizes one stage in that phenomenon of transformation, of slow organic change, with which as spiritual beings we are free to co-operate or which we may resist or retard. This stage of conflict is the one in which mankind at the moment is acutely and even desperately involved. But it can be outgrown. For head and heart are not innately opposed. They belong to each other as the surface of a pool belongs to its depths. They agree together in the physical man in whom the sympathetic and the cerebral nervous systems harmoniously combine. And this harmony is reaffirmed in the spiritual man on a higher level. For the soul, when it is freed from the bondage of the senses, is able to enter into the soul of everything it encounters by its power of universal feeling and by the creative intelligence which informs it and which gives shape and meaning to what it feels.

To think and feel creatively, at once losing and finding the self in what it contemplates, so that it both is and knows its object, is to realize the unity of love and light. For the warmth of love is the glow of the light within it. Such imaginative insight differs from escape into a dream world by being related as patiently as any scientific analysis to the phenomenon of earthly life. But its relation is total and intimate, where that of natural science is external and partial. Such imagination re-creates the persons and things it contemplates. It sees them as wholes and as part of a greater whole. It understands them by entering into conscious communion with them.

This finding of the universal in the particular is the true goal of the mystical life. It is not to be reached by any premature immersion of the self in some limitless "all". To enter the Silence and accept its Void, as I have tried to make clear, is something quite distinct from this. Not an "all" but a "nothing" is what we experience in the Silence, the nothing of that multiple self to which we habitually cling. Indeed the experience of the Silence is no more than a consummation of that deliberate effort after detachment from self in the daily task of human living without the practice of which we should never be qualified to cross the threshold of the inner world.

In the Silence that detachment is carried further until a space begins to open within, devoid of self, into which the light and love of the creative power can flow without hindrance. This is the "non-being in the middle of one's being" of which the Chinese sage spoke. And in course of time, as he added, "it is as if, in the middle of the non-being, there were a being" – the real being of the integrated man.

But this organic change happens, like all other organic changes, "in course of time". It has to be fostered by a constant deepening of our awareness of the inner life which pulses at the heart of the outer world, so that the Silence of that inner space from which speech receives its meaning may become established as an inherent quality of our being and the pure Void from which all our thoughts and actions flow. By practising recollection and detachment we shall cease to be at the mercy of outer or inner distractions and through sympathy towards others' needs and natures we shall offer to the world around us the love which we are receiving from the unseen. For the divine Mind is the source of love within us. When we

[160]

lose touch with that, the light of love goes out or is submerged in the blind onrush of life.

In all this there will be less and less of that laboured self-discipline, with its reward in a sense of acquired merit, which is as alien to love as it is characteristic of morality. For as the creative spirit enters our souls, we discover that its "yoke is easy", its service a perfect freedom from moral cramp. The fruit of this spirit, as St Paul wrote, is "love, joy, peace, long-suffering, gentleness, goodness, faith, meekness, temperance". These are not the constituents of a moral code, imposed with difficulty upon a recalcitrant self, but the innate qualities of a nature transformed from within. The wonder of love is that he who truly loves gives all and sacrifices nothing. For to give all is to be received and given by life itself.

Then only are we heart-whole, because all our faculties of feeling and intelligence are re-united in that Heart of hearts in Which love and light are one. When we are obedient to the light of love which inspires all creation, however imperfectly as yet it may manifest on certain levels through the resistance of matter and the human will, we are informed by a power which ultimately resolves all conflict. And the soul, when it fully awakes to its spiritual nature, can know no greater joy than to express this transforming power which is its innermost light.

Joy, indeed, is the pure essence of the spirit. The soul, which grows through gathering experience, is conversant with and committed to the sorrow and pain of existence. But its reward for all the suffering it has to endure and share in its struggle to be consciously at one with its divine source is a deepening and more constant capacity for joy. This joy is the soul's response to the light within it which irradiates the world which it contemplates, even when that world is dark and sombre. We have only to consider how different the world looks for most of us from hour to hour or it may be from moment to moment, as the quality and focus of our seeing changes, to recognize that consciousness is the light by which we live and the measure of our bondage or our freedom. When its rays are dimmed within us, we see only a world of dense matter, peopled with automatons or with enslaved and blindly struggling creatures, or a colourless, neutral world, as mechanically indifferent to us as we are indifferent to it. But how otherwise it is, when the light, if only for a brief season, breaks through the fleshly or mental veil, as in the first rapture of a love which dreams that it has found its perfect object, as, indeed, love always does.

Then all is changed and we cry with Shakespeare's Miranda:

> *O wonder!*
> *How many goodly creatures are there here!*
> *How beauteous mankind is! O brave new world,*
> *That has such people in it!*

No longer are we exiles from our true home, sitting in tears by the waters of Babylon, sick at heart with remembrance of Zion. But to maintain that vision in a world in which the form and the conduct of mankind are so often far from beauteous and the ubiquity of pain is all that the Buddha said it was, is only possible when we have truly awakened spiritually from the sleep of the senses and our own sickness of soul.

Then, though we shall still be sensitive to the tormented flux of existence in which, on the temporal surface, we participate, we shall draw upon the selfless insight and awareness which is native to the soul when it is free to reflect the pure intelligence which informs it. For when soul and spirit are at one in us, we feel by an act of spontaneous sympathy our identity with all that is struggling, however blindly or perversely, to express the infinite reason of its being and to fulfil the particular part allotted to it in the divine plan for the universe.

LOVE SET FREE

Spiritual or imaginative discernment both feels and knows. This and only this is the true wisdom of which the genius of love consists, when it is re-born in total humility beyond the conflict and complexities which the bound self projects into and extracts from its surroundings – a love that is as simple and as subtle as life, when we allow it to unfold its purpose from within, and as penetrating in its healing rays as the sun, when it re-creates from darkness the miracle of a new world which, though infinitely diverse, is infinitely one.

❖

CHAPTER EIGHT

Realization

1

From what I have already written it will have become clear that as we grow in the experience and art of living from within, we are learning what it means consciously to BE while we move in a stream of becoming. It is this Being which the Silence infuses into our soul from a spiritual source at its centre and which harmonizes our various faculties. Previously much of our life has been a struggle to impress ourselves on our world and particularly on those whom we want to please or whom we fear or covet or dislike. This desire which, in the form of ambition, can spur to laudable achievement or even to creative enterprise, is natural enough. But it easily grows morbid, because it springs from a sense of deficiency which we try to counter by self-assertion. Fulness of being is beyond our power to command or impose. It is given to those who have found the way into what is real in themselves and in others. And the incessant strife and contention which trouble the world is due to man's lack of trust in the Reality to which he belongs and by virtue of which each one of us, uniquely and unfathomably, IS.

We cannot transgress the wholeness of things without becoming lopsided and the greater our worldly success may be, the deeper, probably, will be our inward failure. Yet it is only when we become painfully conscious of this failure that we are likely to abandon compromise and work patiently on ourselves to reverse the childish habit

[164]

of trying to impose on reality. Then it can become possible to enter into a right relationship with life and to realize what it means to be constantly renewed in the spirit.

But claims to such renewal are often made far too easily by people who have experienced some kind of emotional release from repressions or inhibitions or who have joined some religious body which gives them a sense of security. For this renewal really to happen the mind has to become silent. It has to withdraw from the world of change and its traffic, so that it can learn to rest in a Consciousness which contains within Itself all possibilities of thought and feeling and a security and peace so mysteriously absolute that in its presence fear is literally unthinkable and joy serenely unconditioned. Few who call upon God or even claim to be inspired by him have really achieved this mind-stilled act of recollection without which the old self still remains secretly in command, braced against what threatens its survival.

True presence of mind consists of an immediate spiritual insight, which is distinct from psychological awareness because it owes nothing to the accumulations of our past experience or to our powers of analysis or deduction. In such insight attention is purely concentrated on the content of the moment, a concentration only possible if we cling neither to ourselves nor to any object. This enables the spirit present in us to irradiate our soul and its sensible faculties with something of its inherent light. It is by thus resting between the eternal wings of the Bird of Life, as an Eastern sage described it, that we regain our true relationship with Nature on the higher level of consciousness and can become creative in all we are and do.

This is the meaning of recollection without which the new life of the spirit, however ardently desired, cannot be sustained or its art learned and practised. In the previous chapter I have tried to show how the mind needs to be reunited with the heart, in which the Light waits to be quickened. The true function of the mind is to quicken this Light in the heart. To act thus it must cease to appropriate the Light for its own uses in its private mental field or in order to further its designs upon life.

It is through the heart that the Light should be mediated to the senses, which will then, in turn, be "informers of the heart", as Traherne called them. But the self-centred mind is ever ready to take a short cut to experience by acting directly on and through the senses, illicitly stimulating them to seize upon the things of the world and heartlessly exploit them. This mental aberration is the cause of all human misery, and recollection alone can undo it. For recollection is primarily the practice of thinking through the heart instead of mentally activating the senses.

The heart in which we need to think and feel and know is not, of course, the heart in which we are agitated by emotions or hunger for possession. Nor is it the physical organ by which we breathe and blood is circulated. We owe life to this heart, but the Light we are seeking, that Light which George Eliot described as "the last refinement of Energy, capable of bathing even the ethereal atoms in its ideally illuminated space", is not an emanation of the physical nor can it be generated by feeling. It is neither enclosed in the body nor limited by any dimension of space and time. It is the light of the spiritual world, the pure consciousness, implicit in life, which both is and acts.

Of this Sun of our being our mind is only a lunar satellite. In the night of the senses we see objects only by the reflected light of the mind which is the moon in our heavens. And seeing thus we see at best "through a glass darkly". But when the sun of our being rises and shines through the heart, we see all things directly from within as vessels of that Light.

This Sun within us makes its presence felt in the inherent desire we all have for self-transcendence, for union and completeness in something which exceeds us and which we truly are. We fret against the bondage under which we live on the physical and psychological levels of our nature and long to transcend them in an awareness which is pure and free. Our ignorant heart, despite its ardent and lively impulses, is neither pure nor free. To receive the Light, it must cease to cling to outer things and must open inwardly to the spiritual world of which, in its pure depths, it is a portal. Then, quickened from within, we begin to know beyond the division of heart and mind.

We are committed, in fact, to a new task of understanding which involves thinking in and with the heart. To "recollect", in its essential meaning, has nothing to do with memory, unless it be to remember a condition of unified being which we may have enjoyed in some heaven we have forgotten. It is to unite thought and feeling in a creative or imaginative act and to practise such an act patiently and persistently until it becomes habitual. So long as we are enslaved by passing time, we cannot hope to penetrate to the level in ourselves where such an intuitive act becomes possible.

For time, as we ordinarily experience it, reflects the degree to which we are separated from our depths and are carried, in a somnolent or feverish acquiescence, on the surface of the stream. True time, as Maurice Nicoll has so revealingly shown,* is something of which the movement from past to future, in which we ordinarily drift and drain away, is only a superficial aspect. Time, in its depth, belongs to another dimension in which, as Rilke sang in one of his "Sonnets to Orpheus", we were still at home in childhood and which persists, deep, quiet and rooted, through all our waxing and waning.

This enduring time revolves round the timeless centre within, which ensures that everything which happens to us or recurs on the temporal circumference of our lives can be felt to be timely because grounded in that deep

* In *Living Time* by Maurice Nicoll.

heart which has its own infallible reason for our being, at any moment, just what and where we are.

It is because we have lost touch with this timeless heart that we live so much in the past or the future in distracted or resentful flight from the NOW, in which past and future meet, not to devour each other, but in a creative embrace constantly renewed from instant to instant. For the future is folded up in the present and unfolds there as the past. But what is passed will unfailingly recur, in the circling of time, as a future waiting to unfold again, until we have wholly absorbed its timeless meaning. Thus in each moment which we fully live we express, in a degree uniquely appropriate to that moment, all that we have been and shall be, and so all that we essentially ARE.

In such moments of constantly renewed re-birth from our timeless centre we are truly present in time and the conflict between the enduring and the transitory is no longer felt. It is this sense of being continually renewed in time from a dimension beyond the temporal that we can recover and strengthen by recollection. In doing so, we shall not only discover a new organ of knowledge, but gain a quite new sense of "I", not as something transient which we must struggle to preserve, but as a focal point of permanent being.

2

If recollection, then, in all its modes and methods, is meant to relate us to what is real in ourselves, realization is an awakened sense of living in the known presence of the real and in union with it. Our first approach to the real is usually through a dawning sense of the unreal in ourselves and in the world about us. The root of our dissatisfaction is the impermanence of everything. Even the presumptive "I" to which we cling is as inconstant as the weather and as changeable as the wind. It is subject to the humours of the body and the caprices of the mind, and is at the mercy of chance, sickness and death. And so is every thing or person to which this "I" attaches itself. Some are more durable than others, but all only wait their time to vanish.

Yet we would not fret at such impermanence or even recognize it, were there not within us a sense of something that is eternal. Religion has given form to this something in the person of God and as children we are encouraged to believe in this person as a mysterious being, other than and outside ourselves, to Whom we can offer petitionary prayers or appeasing sacrifices and from whom we may ultimately receive the gift of eternal life in a heaven which will differ from earth only in being perfectly adapted to give endless satisfaction to our more elevated impulses. But, in fact, this august Person is seldom more real to us than a constitutional monarch or a great-grandfather whose formidable character still haunts the memory of his family.

Men's conception of such a God, of his qualities and powers, will, of course, vary greatly from the crude to the refined according to their spiritual development. But all theism assumes that God is a being other than his worshippers, however close they may come to him, and that he possesses the reality and permanence which they lack in themselves and seek unavailingly in the world.

This is true enough of the "I" which is divided by its self-centredness from real being. Yet the personal qualities with which the theist invests his God are all derived from what he knows of his own nature, only magnified and idealized. His "Thou art" is another and better way of saying "I am". There is, of course, the transcendental element in his faith, the *"mysterium tremendum"* behind the Person, the Godhead behind the God. But this, too, is conceived in the depths of himself, is the hidden genius working in the unfathomable mines of his nature or, as an

6*

elemental force, links him, through his instincts, with the primordial life of the physical world.

All that he regards as objective in God is, at different depths in himself, subjective in origin. The Creator whom he worships must transcend and surpass his partial self. Nevertheless his God is as much his creation as his creator. And it is primarily because he has lost touch with what he really is or has yet to discover it that he needs to create a Deity other and truer than he is, to Whom he may aspire and by whom he may be judged, instructed and ultimately forgiven.

In philosophical terms, therefore, theism implies dualism. And Christianity in particular, despite its doctrine of the trinity, has always resolutely opposed a non-dual view of reality. But non-dualism does not involve a refusal to recognize the dual process, the meeting of contraries, which governs all creation. It involves only a recognition of the Unity in which all possible contraries, and particularly that of subject and object, are grounded and in which they can be creatively reconciled.

How then does this affect our conception of God and the kind of devotion which may ultimately lead to realization? The more external the God we worship is to ourselves, the more he reflects the lack of inwardness in his worshipper and the separation between subject and object which is characteristic of the divided self. But the more deeply we feel our way into ourselves, the less do we experience God as an external authority watching over us with an omniscient and judicial eye. We recognize that we are still imperfectly related to reality through wilful impulses. But we recognize, too, that this relationship will never be fulfilled by a life-time of prayers and sacrifices offered to an outside deity.

This does not mean that we must necessarily cease to give any form to the reality with which we long to be united. For just as God, conceived as the source and fount of the real, creates himself in the true form of each of us, so we can create a likeness of him through the power of inward vision with which he has endowed us. But the image of him which we create will be true or false, whole or partial, to the exact degree to which we are inwardly enlightened. The God of the ethical or intellectual dualist, however edifying, reflects his moral and mental limitations and fails as an image of the real and a means of communion with it. To be in communion with God is to commune with our real Self and is only possible to the degree that we have discovered that Self. In giving form to reality and naming it God, we may celebrate the greatness or grace of his Person, as an artist might do. But all such forms are relative to ourselves. They image more or less truly That which is without form, in which we eternally have our being.

It is through this formless ground of unity, at once transcendent and present in each of us, that "you" and "I" as distinct individuals, can meet in creative relationship. Equally "God" and "I", if God is conceived as a sublime person confronting or towering over me, can only enter into communion through the same uncreated ground. Unless united in this, we must remain separate, if not painfully at variance.

The worship, then, of God which all religions regard as of the first importance will not necessarily lead to realization. Indeed of itself it obviously seldom does, unless the devotion implicit in it is so intense and pure and so faithfully sustained that what divides the worshipper from the object of his worship is ultimately effaced. Devotion is an end in itself. It is, also, a means to an end. It takes us out of ourselves, as does all activity to which we give ourselves whole-heartedly, but it can also help us to find our Self. Ideally to love is to be united wholly with life in the very centre of our being. But this is only possible when no tremor of distraction disturbs us. Public worship or rituals seldom have the power so completely to deliver us from our own unrest and even private devotion will fail in its concentration until the mind has been brought under control.

There are many methods and exercises which may help us in acquiring this control. The complete suspension of unreal thought and uncentred feeling which is the aim of them all is not an end in itself, but the condition of a new kind of consciousness and a new responsiveness to life. Patanjali, the Indian sage, described concentration as "holding the mind within a centre of spiritual consciousness in the body, or fixing it on some divine form, either within the body or outside it". But whatever it be upon which we concentrate our attention, whether some concrete thing or some inward quality in which we are deficient, or some suffering person towards whom we direct our love and sympathy, we are learning thereby to extricate ourselves from the psychological ferment of egoism and so opening up the ground of our being in which creative life has its roots.

Meditation to be fruitful must be more than an exercise. It must be an art and as such is of value not only in concentrating the mind simultaneously in ourselves and upon one object, but in deepening our relationship until we begin to share our identity with what we contemplate, entering into it subjectively and receiving it as a subject into ourselves. In such experience we begin to realize, however imperfectly, what union means and how it involves the ultimate extinction of the false "I" whose distracted or desirous mind multiplies alien objects around it.

This initiation into a new kind of relationship, to which meditation leads, as it deepens, cannot fail to affect our conception of God, the pure and central object of all contemplation. Less and less shall we think of him as a projected figure. More and more shall we experience him inwardly even when we contemplate some image of his Being.

REALIZATION

In the Christian faith Jesus is the divinely human mediator who makes it possible for "the second man, the Lord from heaven", in St Paul's words, to be born within us, replacing the first earth-bound Adam. For this "second man" God is no longer an object, but a spirit. He is his prime Subject and his very Self.

Yet most Christians reject Jesus's assurance that the way to union with their divine source is directly open to them and insist that salvation depends on belief in Jesus as a personal and historical saviour and is a consequence of the unique sacrifice which he made.

Eastern faiths, on the other hand, declare that the divine incarnates in all those Perfected Souls who enter into conscious union with their source. Devotion offered to such a "Realized Man" is regarded as an important and, in most cases, essential preliminary aid to spiritual enlightenment, but no more than that. For invaluable as the inspiration of such a "revealer of the path" can be, it is always insisted that the real Master is within the seeker himself and that the human Master and teacher exists only to help his devotee by the quickening power and example of his attainment.

Devotion to God, therefore, conceived as a sublime object of worship can gradually deepen, as Self-knowledge grows, into a realization that the God of our imaginings is a projected figure of the One indwelling Spirit. When we can affirm that Spirit with an immediate awareness beyond mental reflection, we shall know that God and we are eternally one in time and beyond it and that all which seems to separate us from him is a mental illusion.

It is this self-begotten illusion and the mental habits associated with it, which devotees seek to destroy by the repetition of *mantras* or invocations of the Divine Name or by loving concentration on some ideal aspect of the Creator as Father or Mother, or by some form of self-forgetfulness in unitive action, whether in disinterested social service or in the practice of an art or of the daily craft of life and its various tasks. All these are means by which devotion may release the deeper being within us from the grip of the ego, and the sense of doing things by our own will may yield to a knowledge that the true actor is the creative will of Life itself and that only in responding and conforming to that will can we experience total peace, freedom and happiness.

We shall not, of course, awaken from illusion through devotional practices, however intense or continuous, unless we, also, practise choiceless awareness in the whole conduct of our lives. The dualist approaches life as a moralist, the non-dualist as an artist. The one strives to control and discipline the self, the other to co-operate with life in a task of re-creation. All true virtues are expressions of the divine order, of the love and law which govern the unseen world and maintain its harmony. But some are more conducive to inward change than others. The positive virtues which appeal most to the strenuous moralist need to be balanced by other qualities which cannot exist without a radical renunciation of self-will. "Moral rearmament" can counter disorder, but will never, in itself, initiate a new order. On the other hand the gentler virtues, sympathy, patience, equanimity, contentment, attentiveness or humility compel a change of rhythm and tempo in our whole being. They are the feminine counterpart of courage, resolution, honesty, decisiveness, adventure, and the like.

The particular value of the passive virtues, which are enduringly positive in their own way, is that, by giving us time to be receptive, they nourish awareness. Without inward and outward awareness, which is the reverse of self-consciousness, love is too blindly impulsive or possessive to free us from ourselves. We cannot know and love another's truth save through the eyes of our own.

Admittedly much that is called self-knowledge is only analysis by the un-enlightened self of its own ignorance

[174]

and, as such, no more than an elaborate exercise in self-absorption and self-deception. True awareness begins where self-engrossment ends. It comes to us not through a willed effort of the mind, directed towards ourselves or another, but by ceasing to manipulate the mind in our own interest or to defend ourselves against our deepest feelings behind a rampart of logic and will. In a mind thus freed from interested control pure consciousness can manifest. Such awareness is not passive reflection, but spiritual perception, vital and immediate.

Until mind and heart are thus released from personal tension in a harmony of knowing and being, no total commitment to life is possible. Those, today, who, in anger or embitterment or a repudiation of spiritual values, preach the necessity of "engagement" are, more often than not, committed only to the flux and conflict of existence and sublimely uncritical of themselves. But in true awareness we are at once sensitively "engaged" in the issues of life and its human drama and recollected in that deep centre of our being in which alone we can really say I AM. Unless we are thus recollected, we cannot redeem the time, however vitally involved in existence or devoted to some form of God we may profess ourselves to be. Nor can we know the eternal gaiety and solemnity at the heart of things.

3

Devotion, then, and Self-inquiry can both lead to a realization of what we truly are, but only if ultimately they merge into each other. As the great Indian sage, Shankara, declared at the beginning of his "Crest Jewel of Wisdom", "a man may study the scriptures, obey the laws, perform religious rites and love and offer sacrifices to the Gods. Yet he will not win Freedom in a thousand years except by knowing his oneness with the Self."

Ramana Maharshi, to whom I referred earlier, defined with characteristic brevity the stages by which this knowledge can be attained. "First," he said, "one sees the Self as objects, then one sees the Self as void, then one sees the Self as Self; only in this last case there is no seeing because seeing is being."

Most people, even among those who recognize that their vision is external and superficial, remain in the first stage in which they see reality more as an object than a subject. If they are religious, they may even condemn any effort to advance beyond it as a transgression of the limits imposed upon human consciousness by God himself. Yet if God is the very core of our being without and separate from whom nothing truly exists, to exclude him, in whatever degree or on whatever grounds, from the inmost citadel of ourselves or to limit our essential identity with him is to deny the totality of his Presence. The man who thinks, says one of the *Upanishads*, "He is one and I another, he knows not."

The ego perpetuates its many selves by fostering this illusion of separateness and by mentally multiplying objects which it can possess or manipulate, but with which it can never intimately unite. For only a Self which we experience, not as another, but as our very being, can unite us inwardly with every manifestation of Itself. The dualist, however, thinks it necessary to maintain a discreet division between seeing subject and object seen, because without it, he supposes, all sense of form would vanish and with it all effective action. But human experience has shown that this need not happen, that, in fact, a non-dual relationship, centred in our own nothingness, which releases in us our creative potentiality, is incomparably richer in shared life and meaning and in fullness of joy and peace than the uneasy tension between "I" and "not-I" which it supersedes.

Admittedly to pass from seeing the Self as we see objects

to "seeing the Self as Self" necessitates a transitional stage when "one sees the Self as void". And it is from this threat of ineffectual and even terrifying emptiness that most people draw back. But the threat, as I have tried to show in a previous chapter, is felt by the ego which fears its own dissolution. It is not the Void which threatens us, but only our recoil from it. For the Void is the Silence in which the mystery of creation and re-creation is continually enacted and to which Krishna directs his disciple in the *Bhagavad Gita*:

> *When all desires are stilled and the mind, withdrawing within, gathers the multitudinous straying senses into the harmony of recollection,*
> *Then, with reason armed with resolution, let the seeker quietly lead the mind into the Spirit, and let all his thoughts be silence.**

Surrender of all self-centred activity of mind and body is the basic condition of experiencing the Void and of receiving its healing and transforming power. For, in Ramana Maharshi's words, "the mind having been differentiated from its true and primal state of Pure Being, which is the Self . . . slips away therefrom and, assuming the form of thought, constantly pursues objects of sense-gratification. Therefore it is assailed by the vicissitudes of life and becomes weak and dispirited."

But recalling the mind to its primal state or, in Krishna's words, "leading it into the Spirit" is a very positive expression of the deep passivity, the acknowledged powerlessness, without which no amount of resolute activity would be of any avail. The ancient method of Self-inquiry, which Ramana Maharshi advocated in the present century, is directed to this end. It involves, as I have shown, a persistent pushing back of self-consciousness upon its source, by which we cease to identify ourselves with the body or

* Translated by Juan Mascaró in *The Bhagavad Gita* (Penguin Classics).

with the picture of what we are which we have mentally formed and to which we continually add throughout our life in the body.

We are fascinated as well as distracted by this picture, with its high lights and shadows and dramatic vicissitudes. But in time we begin to tire of the spectacle and even to wish to dissociate ourselves from it. And it is then, as we withdraw our gaze momentarily from what Plato described in his memorable myth as the shadows on the wall of our cave, that the question "What am I?" can arise in our minds. The fact that we can ask such a question is itself proof that we are something other than the flux of impressions and sensations or the nexus of thoughts in which we have merged our identity. We cannot be as ephemeral as these since we can watch them come and go.

And if we persist in our questioning and our watching, we find that something deep within us equally refuses to accept the suggestion that what we are is a shadow without substance. If there is one thing which we can never really doubt despite all our self-questioning or self-denying, it is the Self-evident fact of our own identity. And the more we gather "the multitudinous senses into the harmony of recollection", the less real do our habitual self or selves seem in the presence of the Being of which we are then conscious. Instead of the egotistic shadow without substance which we can shed as a snake sheds its skin, this newly-discovered Being is a substance without shadow.

Of course we shall never find ourselves at this depth if, in pursuing our Self-inquiry, we maintain our old habits of external thinking. We can expect no fruitful answer in this subjective field of inquiry from what Wordsworth called "the niggling intellect". Indeed we have not begun to ask the question with the necessary humility and openness so long as the "I" that asks can continue to argue about itself. All such self-involved dialogue can only perpetuate the divided state which it reflects. However insistently the bound "I" asserts or tries to deny itself, it cannot timelessly say I AM, because it exists only as a vanishing point in the passage of time. Unless we are ready to receive the answer to our question from a timeless plane of our being, we waste time in asking it.

Of that hidden place in which reality reveals itself the *Chandogya Upanishad* declares: "Within the city of Brahman, which is the body, there is the heart, and within the heart there is a little house. This house has the shape of a lotus and within it dwells that which is to be sought after, inquired about, and realized." Or, in the words of the *Mundaka Upanishad*: "In the effulgent lotus of the heart dwells Brahman, passionless and indivisible. He is pure. He is the light of all lights. The knowers of Brahman attain him."

The language is necessarily figurative, since only images can embody the beauty and mystery of the spiritual Kingdom. It is to this Kingdom and the creative power within it that the practice of Self-inquiry can open a way by leading us to a point within ourselves from which we can see through the compulsive masquerade of our personality and its outer life and detach ourselves from it. Then a new life can begin to grow from a true depth of being, in which our mind will cease to multiply alien objects and be related once again to its pure Subject which, as the primal "I" of creation, is the source of all we are. We are drawn back to the hidden ground in which our sense of distinctive being originates, and in which it is maintained. We begin, then, to realize what I AM means. It is as if I AM is said within us by That which eternally is and by virtue of which we eternally are. We become in that moment part of the total affirmation of life in which the I AM of creation and the I AM of ourselves is one.

When the ego says "I am", it asserts itself at the expense of someone or something and has to go on asserting itself if it is not to be engulfed in the mere movement of life.

But the "I" which affirms us and which we consentingly affirm in the depth of our being when we truly say I AM, has no beginning and no end. Past and future co-exist in its eternal NOW. We carry both within us and in the cyclic movement of true time our future is as much behind us as before. By affirming this "I", by a spiritual, not a mental, act, we really are and know that we are. As this affirmation becomes established in us, the shadow of the ego fades away and the conflict inherent in it between self and non-self and between its own divided impulses is resolved in what Coleridge called "the eternal act of creation in the infinite I AM". We realize then the truth of the ancient Gnostic saying, "I am thou and thou art I and wheresoever thou art, I am there; in all I am scattered, and whenceso-ever thou willest, thou gatherest Me; and gathering Me, thou gatherest Thyself."*

Since the absolute Reality, from which every form derives is itself without name and form, it might be thought that communion with it would entail only the bliss of a formless ecstasy or a total absorption and abstraction in the realm of the unconditioned, hardly distinguishable from cataleptic trance. Certain kinds of super-consciousness, as practised in the East, have seemed to confirm this idea. But the true teachers have never approved it. There have, indeed, been exceptional men, such as Sri Rama-Krishna in the last century, who frequently passed into a blissful subjective state in which he was oblivious of his surroundings. But when he emerged from it, he had much to give through the very intensity of such timeless communion with his spiritual source.

In the East such exceptional men have always been regarded as light-houses or power-houses through whom the vibration of the higher or more interior realms might pass to those capable of receiving it. But such states are

* From *The Gnostic Gospel of Eve*. Quoted by G. R. S. Meed in *Fragments of a Faith Forgotten*.

easily parodied by charlatans exploiting the ignorance of the multitude or merely by fugitives from human responsibilities and relationships. If "realization" consisted only of this, how barren of fruit in this life it would be and how much of human experience would be left unredeemed by understanding.

Self-affirmation does not involve the annihilation or suspension of our human faculties, but their organic coordination. The eternal "I" is both unconditioned and creative. It is creative because it is unconditioned, being thereby free to relate itself absolutely to every form of its creation. "Not a sparrow can fall without your Father." And we, too, in the degree to which we develop the capacity, so simple and so difficult, to be what we truly are, enter inevitably into fuller and deeper relationship with every form of life. No one is more wholly Self-possessed than he who has dissociated himself from his body and its desires and from all the conditioned thoughts which distract. But it is a Self-possession which unites us with the whole world through the light of meaning which has dawned in our hearts. That dawning of meaning has been well described by Maurice Nicoll:

There can suddenly be opened within the heart or in the mind a realm of experience that is not the external world (though it may interpenetrate it) and we are then bathed in the light of meaning – in that light without violence, which is pure experience, luminosity without shadow, in which the hardness of self vanishes. We see: with the authority that meaning gives us. We feel; in depth, without talking to ourselves, without the mirror of surface personality. Every experience of that light deeply creates us. It is creating light, transforming meaning, which all have sought since the beginning of time, light that can do no violence to anyone, meaning that shows us what we have always known and never

had the strength to remember. Not only do we feel our-
selves created by every experience of that light, but this,
we say, is what we are always looking for – this meaning
and reality, this bliss that we have misinterpreted and
sought in a thousand useless physical directions – this
is what we all desire, which the outer light of life pre-
tends to offer, but never properly gives, this union which
we perceive really is union, the secret idea behind our
*odd, searching, incomplete lives.**

To receive this light of meaning and union involves a
total break with our old attitude to the world and our old
habits of thought and feeling. When we begin to live in
and by the Spirit, heart and mind are responsive to its
will and its consciousness, which relate us to the world in
which we live in a new way. To the heart purified by spiritual intelligence the within and the without are seen to be
aspects of One being. The world is no longer a world of
divided objects, but of related forms in which each form
is a whole and also part of a greater whole. In the words
of the *Bhagavad Gita*:

When one sees Eternity in things that pass away and
infinity in finite things, then one has pure Knowledge.
But if one merely sees the diversity of things, with their
diversions and limitations, then one has impure know-
ledge.
And if one selfishly sees a thing as if it were everything,
independent of the ONE and the many, then one is in
the darkness of ignorance.†

In spiritual vision we see imaginatively, giving form to
That which in formless essence we are whether, like the
child, William Blake, we see God's forehead pressed
against the window-pane or recreate the world around

* From *The Mark* by Maurice Nicoll.
† As translated by Juan Mascaró in Penguin Classics.

REALIZATION

us as a revelation of the Unity and relationship which
emanate from its unseen Principle. Thus in the light of meaning the illusion of separation
between self and not-self is dissipated. Only in appearance
is "the other" in any of its forms alien to us. In reality the
world is within us as we are within the world. Knowing
this, we can abandon our defences and be infinitely
hospitable to experience, being at home to everything
which presents itself to us. As Krishna declares in the
Gita:

*He sees himself in the heart of all beings and he sees
all beings in his heart. This is the vision of the liberated
man, a vision which is ever one.*

*And when he sees me in all and he sees all in me, then
I never leave him and he never leaves me.*

4

The man who has found his true being and begun to live
in it may not be recognizable outwardly as distinct from
his fellows. But inwardly he has a special task, determined
by what he is. Life develops from its lower to its higher
levels through the growth, not of outer knowledge, but
of inward consciousness. And such insight is the fruit of
obedience to the creative spirit within. It ripens thus on
the tree of each life which is truly rooted and cultivated.
If we are obedient to the Spirit which knows and loves, we
receive inspiration and direction from super-human levels
in the unseen through the higher centres in ourself. We
may or may not be conscious of being so overshadowed, but
no one who has lived the life of the spirit at all intimately
can doubt the reality, not only of an enlightening Presence,
but of informing presences, whether we name them Master
or guardian angel or advanced souls on our ray of life, or
acknowledge only their anonymous influence.

To realize our identity with universal Being is to enlarge the whole range of our contacts with the cosmos. We are no longer earth-bound within the confines of our physical senses, though these senses continue to relate us to our physical environment and the more effectively for being integrated in a greater whole. Through participating in this whole we awake to the truth that we are the meeting place of two worlds and that humanity's unique task is to carry forward the redemption of earth by heaven, of the outward by the inward, the material by the spiritual, a task in which we need the aid of those more advanced beings in the unseen who, at different levels of spiritual unfoldment and in bodies of finer texture, can transmit light to our higher senses.

To receive this light we need to be open and, as I have stressed, selflessly silent. But our task does not end there. As we receive from above or within, so are we called to give light to those levels upon which life is struggling upwards out of darkness. The genius of the spirit, as we discover it, in ourselves, is to transform. As new-born children and trustees of it, that is supremely our task. The poet, Rilke, was deeply convinced of this and wrote in one of his letters:

Transitoriness is everywhere plunging into a profound Being. And therefore all the forms of the here and now are not merely to be used in a time-limited way, but, so far as we can, instated within those superior significances in which we share. . . . To instate what is here seen and touched within the wider, within the widest orbit – that is what is required. Not within a Beyond, whose shadow darkens the earth, but within a whole, within the Whole. Nature, the things we move about among and use, are provisional and perishable; but so long as we are here, they are our possession and our friendship, sharers in our trouble and gladness, just as

they have been the confidants of our ancestors. There-
fore, not only must all that is here not be corrupted or
degraded, but, just because of that very provisionality
they share with us, all these appearances and things
should be comprehended by us in a most fervent under-
standing and transformed. Transformed? Yes, for our
task is to stamp the provisional, perishing earth into
ourselves so deeply, so painfully and passionately, that
its being may rise again, "invisibly" in us. We are the
bees of the invisible.

This is the creative meaning of "reverence for life",
which is not a mere avoidance of wanton or selfish destruction, but a sharing with life all that we have to give and
are ready to receive. Such reverence can only become a
spontaneous act when we have come to see all the forms of
the here and now as essentially part of ourselves within
the whole. To Rilke the lower kingdoms of nature, the
flower and the creature, made a special appeal for compre-
hension and inclusion in human understanding. But our
own weaker brethren have, perhaps, an even stronger
claim. Those who are bewildered or frustrated, sunk in
ignorance or in painful conflict with themselves or their
fellows, will be comprehended in a new way by the man
or woman in whom spiritual perception has replaced self-
interest in all its forms, mental, moral or material.

Such perception, in all but a few, will always be imperfect
on this earth. The supreme attainment, the complete
merging in the central light of unconditioned Being, were
it possible, would blind the aspirant who sought it prematurely or with impure motives. And the very few who have
hitherto enjoyed that ultimate experience, beyond thought
and beyond words, have transcended the human condition
as we know it, in order to minister to it.

But for those whose task it is to strip off the veils of
ignorance and insensibility which, at different levels of

their being, obscure the Light within them, realization, once the awakening has occurred, is a progressive thing. And it grows, not only through the subjective discipline by which our spiritual faculties are trained and developed, but by the deepening and perfecting of relationship. Real relationship is impossible until we are sufficiently concentrated within not to be helplessly conditioned by outer things. It is for this that we work in the Silence. But the impact of our environment is almost equally important in putting us to the test, in habituating us to deal calmly and resolutely with obstacles and hostile forces, to cultivate patience and equanimity in the face of failure or defeat, and, above all, in measuring our capacity to discriminate between the unreal and the real.

Such discrimination involves a sustained awareness, not of the superficial aspect of things upon which self-interest fastens or over which it flickers, but of the pure quality inherent in every manifestation of life in which we participate. Relationship differs from mere sociability in establishing, at whatever level, a vital contact, a mutual recognition. To recollect the real, moment by moment, in the meeting of self and not-self, we need to be instated in the whole within which we are relaxed and attentive. In such effortless and sympathetic attention creative insight can grow, until, to quote from a novel by Stella Zilliacus, "all prejudices and artificial barriers vanish, and only the essence of people and things remains, so that a powerful current of goodness flows unimpaired."

To be related is to be in harmony in all our experience with the unifying forces of life through being obedient to the idea which informs them. The physical substance of everything, in the particular form which it assumes, is transitory. But its form is the expression of an idea which determines all the superficial changes which its form undergoes and which survives the death of the vehicle which it animates. This idea is, indeed, its true

[186]

form of which its body as grasped by the senses is a passing reflection.

To deepen and refine our perception of this true form in everything and so to commune with the essence of people and things, not by a denial or disregard of their earthly features, but by seeing and loving them from within is at once the task and the reward of realization, when the recollection which has been established in the Silence expands to contain the outer world.

To see someone or something spiritually is not to have an idea or ideas about them. Nor is it to idealize them, in the common meaning of the word. For that is only to speculate or sentimentalize from outside. When we do this, we have lost touch with our own depths and so cannot see into the kindred depths of what we contemplate. It is by seeing into our own nature and finding there the eternally present I AM which underlies and gives meaning to all appearances, that we are delivered from the false and superficial notion of ourselves and from the mental prison which is composed of such notions. By the power of this true idea of our own being we are free to see into the real nature of others and to love without envy or desire what we see.

Every genuine gift of ourselves to life must be unconditional, because life itself originates in the unconditioned. But this does not mean that spiritual vision overlooks the particular form or conditions under which any created being manifests. Love does not consume the finite in the infinite, but unites them. Its sensitiveness to the surface of life and to the felicities of its forms is heightened and deepened by the Void in which it is rooted. Too often religious belief, like rationalism, is associated with a conventional or atrophied sense of beauty. But for the creative spirit truth is inseparable from beauty. To see anything truly is to comprehend it as a perfectly related whole. Beauty is born of thus looking into the soul of things, of seeing them undividedly. When the awakened spirit contemplates an object, it enters into communion with it and the meaning which is born of that communion manifests in the beauty of its true form.

To experience what is real, we must see and feel the emptiness of the phenomenal world and its multiple lures. But out of the void thus realized springs a regenerated vision of a world which embodies meaning and mystery in every crystallized particular and in which nothing is basically unrelated or unredeemable by the love which both acts and understands. What had become dead through familiarity and stock associations is suddenly alive and new.

Spiritual vision is constant. For it is the vision of the infinite in the finite, of the Eternal One uniquely present in ourselves and in all else. Such vision is hard to attain; harder still to sustain, amid the psychological and physical strains and stresses of circumstance and the agitated flux of life. But if we can hold to That in ourselves which abides within all the forms it creates and destroys, the events of time no longer blind and bewilder. Even while we are involved in their actuality, we see them imaginatively. Then the earthly flux falls into a meaningful pattern, stretched between the great contraries of hell and heaven. In the natural process we perceive the outworking of inner laws and in the fleeting form the image of a timeless truth and of a beauty that cannot die. The body of life is no longer opaque, but transmits its indwelling light in the pure gradations of colour which enchant the senses. In each particular manifestation we feel the pure idea which animates it, the heavenly azure in the changing blue of the sky, the absolute pitch within each note of the scale, the holiness of the heart's affections sanctifying the delight of the senses, the golden wisdom ready to disperse the shadows from the aspiring mind, the omnipresent Being which enfolds in its peaceful benediction all the outward turmoil and travail of existence.

Such is the new world of finer apprehension which

awaits us if we can truly see into ourselves and, by affirming the heaven within, redeem the hell which we have in
part inherited and in part perpetuated through our own
ignorance and perversity. For to see through division and
the desecration which it inflicts on life is to know with
William Blake that everything which lives is holy and, as
such, to be loved and shared and infinitely enjoyed. But
without that inward awakening we shall remain ineffectually blind to the real world and its glory, however morally
earnest we may be or religiously inclined to do God's will.

The false world is within us and, by reflection, in all
about us. It is a world in which reality is divided and distorted, but in which the spirit has lost none of its infinite
power to redeem and recreate. By conscious effort in
surrender and affirmation, by continually recognizing our
unreal self and dying to it, we can identify our being with
that power and realize the immediacy of the Divine
Presence of which Traherne wrote: "From the centre to
the utmost bounds of the everlasting hills all is Heaven
before God and full of treasure; and he that walks like God
in the midst of them, is blessed."

The whole struggle of the soul, here on earth, is to cast
off the false mental limitations which ignorance has imposed upon it and to embrace in itself both heart and mind.
For when the mind consents to be the intelligence within
the heart, it is no longer the enemy of the real. And the
ideas which are generated within a heart so enlightened
are spiritual forces which descend into the sick body of
life, charged with the radiations of a higher wisdom and a
creative love. We realize then, in Shelley's words, "how
little yet how great we are", since we can lose ourselves
in That by which the crooked places are made straight and
the captives set free.

CHAPTER NINE

Living and Dying

1

"Time," said Thomas Mann on his eightieth birthday, "works for all of us if only we will allow it to do its work of moulding and raising opposites to a higher unity, and if we will make it fruitful by working on ourselves. Time is a precious gift, handed to us so that in it we may become wiser, better, riper, more nearly perfect. A man who has lived his fourscore years here below knows something about time and the patience that makes time bear fruit. Time is grace." More succinctly William Blake declared that "time is the mercy of eternity".

But for time to be grace or mercy its bond of union with eternity must be cherished. And the same is true of death, which serves time so faithfully. Modern life has become a battle against both time and death. Never, perhaps, has mankind striven harder to escape from time or the recollection of death than today. For millions of people life has become a hectic race against time, a race which must fail, since the faster we run or are mechanically propelled, the less capable we are of coming level with time and absorbing all it has to give and teach us.

Yet behind and beneath this mania for speed, all unconsciously, is a perverse hunger for the timeless, a desire to break through the time-barrier, as through the space and sound barriers, into some unlimited realm. The "I", which cannot transcend itself, tries thus to outrun itself and its tensions and find oblivion in the extreme of meaningless

[190]

motion. The idealist who is contemptuous or impatient of
the actual is, on a higher level, under a like compulsion.
But what lures him is not the oblivion of infinite motion,
but the intoxication of pure abstraction.

Both the idealist and the materialist, in their different
ways, do violence to time and deprive death of its meaning.
But time and death are not mere contingencies to be defied
or disregarded for as long as possible. They are the very
warp of our earthly existence on which the woof of its
meaning is woven. Or, to change the metaphor, from the
moment of our birth death is the soil in which our life
grows and time is the gardener who will cultivate the soil
well or ill according as we employ him wisely. The unearthly seed of our being, sown in this soil, contains within
it an ideal potentiality of growth and of grace. But without
the aid of time and death this growth can never be fulfilled
and it will be stunted in so far as we spurn that aid or fail
to make it our own.

The fulness of being for which we all hunger can never
be experienced by those who view life as an endless
battle against death and regard those who would make
friends with death as traitors to the cause of life. For so
long as we breathe, we live by dying. To live in defiance
of death is as foolish as to hold our breath for fear of losing
it. By championing life against death, by trying to force
them apart and attach ourselves to one of them, we reduce
life to the measure of our own impotence. We reject the
rhythm of Creation, the condition of its renewal.

Life on the physical level is an endless struggle in which
the weaker die. But this is a struggle of life with life, not of
life with death. Life maintains and perpetuates itself by
such struggle, but also by instincts of co-operation which
prevent the struggle from ever proving fatal to the evolution of life as a whole or even to those species which are
necessary to this evolution. In this struggle death is a mode
of life. And so it is on whatever level life manifests.

But in the minds of self-conscious men death has become an enemy. And truly enough it is an enemy assured of victory over those who fear or deny it. Their lives are infected by death instead of being renewed and purified by it and the very stimulants or opiates which they regard as necessary to lighten the burden of living betray how deadly life can become. For life can, indeed, be more deadly than death, as Henry Miller has written.

We cannot be absolute for life unless we are, also, like the duke in Shakespeare's *Measure for Measure*, "absolute for death". We are in fact always dying but always with reservations which diminish, if they do not destroy, the virtue of the act. In some moment of sudden rapture our reservations may be swept away and we may experience, if only partially and sensationally, the ecstasy of dying into the arms of life.

But to make this experience basic to our lives, until it informs and transforms our smallest act, we need to make friends with death. We need to recollect and welcome its presence, to respond gratefully to its working in the hidden places of our being, and, little by little, to come to know and be known by it as lovers know each other. Self-love resists what it regards as such treasonable association with death with all the little life which it has appropriated to itself. It parades its fear of death as a love of life, disguises its misery behind a grinning mask and clings with defiant zest to the wheel of desire-impelled action on which it is endlessly enslaved.

For since life and death unite in the heart of being, we cannot turn against one without alienating the other. When we reject death, the roots of our life begin to die. We become conscious of death merely as destruction, as a force that insidiously saps our vitality or openly menaces it. We defy it, because we fear it and as our fear grows and becomes habitual, so does our estrangement. But in regarding death as some external enemy which we have to fight we are engaged in a war in which our eventual defeat is certain. For death is merciless only to those who set their face against it. In its heart is compassion, the tenderness which speaks in Schubert's song, *"Der Tod Und Das Madchen"* ("Death and the Maiden"). "Give me thy hand," says death to the pleading girl:

> *thou fair, thou little one,*
> *Take courage now, and hush thy weeping.*
> *I am a friend thou need'st not shun:*
> *These arms shall fold thee softly sleeping.*

Those whose work has made them familiar with death-beds agree in saying that the dying, in the last stages of their withdrawal from life, with few exceptions find death to be indeed a friend they need not shun. The death agony is a reflex action of the body and only the soul which clings tenaciously to the physical need be involved in it, because, by doing so, it prevents the process of gradual release into the spiritual world which death intends. In this there is a likeness between the travail, difficult or easy, of child-birth and that of death.

To fight death to the last gasp is natural to the body and those who continue throughout their lives to identify themselves with their body are ill-prepared for the moment when they must leave it. In many cases, of course, suffering gives warning of death's approach and breaks down, in different degrees, a life-time's habit of resistance. The verses from Ecclesiasticus, which Brahms set to music in one of his *"Lieder und Gesange"*, express poignantly the normal human attitude:

> *O death, how bitter art thou unto him that dwelleth in peace, to him that hath joy in his possessions, and liveth free from trouble, to him whose ways are prosperous in all things, to him that still may eat! O death, how welcome thy call to him that is in want and whose*

[193]

7

strength doth fail him and whose life is but a pain, who
hath nothing to hope for and cannot look for relief!
O death, how welcome art thou! How welcome is thy call!

This is the common way in which the presence of death
is mediated to men by the breakdown of their physical
powers or the onset of incurable disease. And for many it
is only when the body fails and physical life loses its
savour, that the soul begins to glimpse through the crumbl-
ing walls of its prison the "country far beyond the stars"
to which it is journeying.

The natural man, secure in his physical strength, remains
a child spiritually. His soul, which is meant to unfold as
the intermediary between earth and heaven, has yet to
open to the divine essence within it and to cast off the
bondage of the earth-bound self. Only as the body approaches death does the soul of such a man begin to awake
from its long sleep and to turn with the unfocussed eyes of
infancy towards the inward world of spirit.

How tenderly Gerard Manley Hopkins depicted such a
man in the sonnet he wrote on "Felix Randal", the "big-
boned, hardy-handsome" farrier, to whom he ministered
in his last days.

Sickness broke him. Impatient he cursed at first, but
mended
Being annointed and all; though a heavenlier heart
began some
Months earlier, since I had our sweet reprieve and
ransom
Tendered to him. Ah, well, God rest him all road ever
he offended.
This seeing the sick endears them to us, us too it endears.
My tongue had taught thee comfort; touch had
quenched thy tears,
Thy tears that touched my heart, child, Felix, poor
Felix Randal;

[194]

LIVING AND DYING

How far from then forethought of, all thy more
  boisterous years,
When thou at the random grim forge, powerful
  amidst peers,
Didst fettle for the great grey drayhorse his bright
  and battering sandal!

The natural man, who associates life so exclusively with
the body, has thus to be broken by age or sickness before
he can begin to turn his inward eyes to that other side of
life which is death and re-birth. In health he seldom thinks
of death but, like the child in Wordsworth's poem, draws
on the zest inherent in life, unconscious that death, even
then, is its renewing principle. To think of death negatively is, indeed, a sign of sickness, of the self-consciousness that splits life in two.

> *Cowards die many times before their deaths;*
> *The valiant never taste of death but once.*

For to live courageously, whether blindly or knowingly,
is to live without self-concern, by the spirit which, undying
in itself, enters into matter to create on the cross of death
and life.

Death, then, as the negative aspect of the impersonal
force we name life, is entirely beneficent in its functions.
But to welcome it into our hearts, to accept it, habitually
and consciously, as an essential mode of real being, we
have to overcome deep-rooted resistances. We have been
so long conditioned to regard our existence here as a fight
for life that we forget that it is not death we must or can
overcome, but our dread of it. What is deadly is not death,
but the state of self-preoccupation in which we ordinarily
live. If we turn our attention to this state and observe
its characteristics, all the effort with which we strive to
preserve ourselves against both life and death can be
expended on the task of removing the causes of our

failure to live trustfully in all the dimensions of our being.

We cannot do this until we are as ready to die as to live, and this means ceasing to cling to any of our possessions, the dearest of which is ourself, or cherish any selfish desire or ambition. How far we are from this readiness we can easily discover by trying to say to ourselves with absolute sincerity, "If I am meant to die today, how happy I shall be, and I entrust to death those whom I love as confidently and ungrudgingly as I entrust myself."

Until we can say this without the slightest twinge of misgiving, we are still imperfectly attuned to life. We flinch from the ultimate sacrifice. Those who, weary of living or broken by sorrow or pain, resign themselves to death, consent to it as the defeated yield to the conqueror. They cannot die affirming the glory of life because their natural eyes are dimmed and their spiritual eyes are not yet opened. To know that glory and to be able to affirm it even when all the glow of earthly life is fading we need to have passed through the initiation of suffering.

Life is suffering, as Gautama declared. Yet few really accept this truth and enter into its meaning. To understand suffering is to understand death. Death is always taking place in and around us, in partings from people and places, in flowers that droop and hopes that fade, in pleasures that pall and in the disillusionment of what we had taken for love. In such moments of change and loss we know the pain of death, but seldom the initiation it offers into reality. To earn this initiation we have to suffer death upon the cross of life at the point within us where the vertical pole of eternal being intersects the horizontal line of temporal existence. Merely to exist, as the word denotes, is to stand outside being, as we move along the horizontal line from past to future. In fact everything subsists in being, but only man can fully realize his being by consciously uniting his existence in time with his eternal essence.

LIVING AND DYING

Physical pain belongs to existence and is life's indication of unbalance or disease. It has to be endured until its immediate cause has been eradicated. But real suffering is other than this. We suffer as spiritual beings who struggle, in our advance along the line of our existence, to rise to a higher level on the pole of our being. For long we thwart the will of life through our inner resistance to its efforts to make us more conscious through the surgery of pain. We react negatively or resentfully to the blows which fall upon us. By thus refusing to assent to the deeper purpose of life in countless thoughts and acts, motivated by fear or greed or blind obstinacy, we establish within us a tightness and a hardness which only suffering can melt.

Creative suffering – and this alone is real suffering – is positively non-resistant. It is a spiritual act, not a physical or mental reaction. And we cannot truly perform it until we wholly consent to the situation in which we find ourselves, however painful or disconcerting it may be, regarding it as the price we must pay for spiritual growth. By thus consenting to suffer we learn how to live by dying, how to surrender our existence to our being, until it is informed, more and more, by the eternal light of our essence.

To suffer thus is to pass through the defensive warfare of pain and pleasure to the pure joy in which we wholly accept and are accepted by life. And this is, also, to live from moment to moment in peaceful communion with death. For only by thus dying to what is resistant in ourselves can we enjoy the inexhaustible originality of life when it is left free to act in us from its true centre.

Life never ceases to offer us occasions for thus "dying in the divine image", to borrow Blake's words, or to remind us how necessary death is to its purposes. Nor are these occasions only those when death casts its shadow on the face of life or another's grief calls for a self-forgetful response. It can be as hard to suffer joy truly as sorrow.

[197]

In thought and theory, too, we may believe, with Whitman, that we are "at peace about God and about death", until a real crisis occurs which threatens our very existence, physically or materially.

For great is the power of the serpent that strives blindly for life in the cave of the instincts until the ignorance of the lower mind is dispersed and its desires are seen for the illusion which they are. Then only does the serpent of life uncoil and, rising out of the darkness into the light, transform the blind instinct in us for physical survival into a clear seeing of the truth which Krishna declares to Arjuna in the second chapter of the *Bhagavad-Gita*:

Interwoven in his creation, the Spirit is beyond destruction. No one can bring to an end the Spirit which is everlasting. . . .
He is never born, and he never dies. He is in Eternity: he is for evermore. Never born and eternal, beyond times gone or to come, he does not die when the body dies. . . .
The Spirit that is in all things is immortal in them all: for the death of what cannot die, cease thou to sorrow.

This Spirit we eternally are. To live this truth is to be enlightened. Time, with its gift of suffering, is our ally in making possible the inner change which leads to such enlightenment. For true suffering opens the channel to spiritual being which our self-centred attachment to natural existence has blocked, and quickens those higher centres in us through which we receive the transforming light of consciousness. The more spiritually alive we are, the more willingly do we die in the act of living and the less does physical death confront us as an enemy that waits to strike.

The body's resistance to death is, of course, natural and it can be safely left to maintain it for as long as is necessary, provided we do not interfere with it. But it is through identifying our spiritual being with this process of nature in the body that we subordinate the immortal in us to the mortal and become a field of conflict. The creative spirit is not at war with death, but with disease on every level. That is the touchstone of its presence. It unites in itself all divided opposites, not by destroying what is distinctive, but by bringing each into a complementary relationship with the other. When we live in and by the spirit which we truly are, the conflict of contraries within us is continually resolved. Life and death are in harmony in a soul and body which are allowed to be obedient to their spiritual principle.

2

There are many methods by which we may foster awareness of our spiritual nature, some of which I have already touched upon. All of them can be seen to involve a break with our habitual mode of living which, from the spiritual standpoint, is a kind of somnambulism. The more we are unconscious, the more are we mechanical. Learning to die means, in the first place, detaching ourselves in spirit from the instinctive, emotional and mental mechanism of the body, while living in it with grace and gratitude, whatever the ordeals through which we may have to pass as a result of being related through the body with the physical world and all that it contains. It is by detaching ourselves from our physical context, not to repudiate, but to observe and understand it, that we can become channels of a spiritual awareness which will enlighten the body's darkness and heal the tensions which self-consciousness has induced.

Identified with the real source of our being, we can descend into our own nature and begin to transform it. Thus to be re-born of the spirit is, also, to be re-born in the flesh. When we live in and by the spirit, death in us is the movement by which life is renewed. But if we cling to the body, it becomes a mere degenerative process.

Those who are strongly attached to the body and the particular play of impulses and reactions which they associate with it will doubtless resist any invitation to detachment as a betrayal of life or as a manichean recoil from the flesh. In support of this they may point to the self-inflicted flagellations of fanatical penitents or to the intensive contemplation of corpses favoured by some Buddhist teachers as a means of killing the love of life. But those who indulge in such practices are still slaves to the body which they castigate or view only under the aspect of physical decay. They are almost as far from inner freedom as the insatiable amorist.

Far from discrediting the body by ceasing to identify ourselves with it we help to rid it of the disease with which we have infected it. Pure life is eternally self-creating and self-renewing and is only sullied by incarnation when we wilfully abuse it. Through this transgression of ours we have lost the art of living and dying from moment to moment in a perpetual affirmation of Being. By identifying ourselves with the body of life in ignorance of its spirit we cannot experience the "Now" in which time and eternity coincide and reality can be fully known and expressed. All the unredeemed antagonisms which afflict and devalue our lives stem from this ignorant attachment to the physical level of our nature.

There can be no escape from this bondage except by an inner awakening. Without that we may speculate about the spiritual or explore the nature of the physical, but we do not build a bridge between them in ourselves. Thus to separate the timeless and its values from the temporal and its contingencies, except as a conceptual convenience by which we may define their relationship, is to make both unreal. A recognition of this has underlain the whole movement in modern philosophy known as "existentialism" and its rejection of all abstract systems of thought divorced from concrete situations. The thinkers of this school differ in many ways, but they agree in insisting that to profess any values is useless unless we have intimately lived and proved them for ourselves.

Yet the values, which we make most deeply our own, are not subject to temporal existence, though we can only test their truth in the changing context of time and place. Courage, generosity, fidelity or compassion, for example, are qualities universally valid, wherever they are encountered and are even dimly or crudely reflected on sub-human levels of life. In their essence they are independent of time and life's real meaning is to be found, not in any sequence of events as such, but in what it contains of such qualities as these, which find distinctive expression and acquire their particular degree of value in a thousand different situations in which the drama of human existence is played out.

To insist on fidelity to existence at the cost of spiritual being, as many "existentialist" writers do, is not to resolve the old conflict between the ideal and the actual. The anti-idealism of this century has been an understandable reaction against the cult of private heavens. The "world of the spirit" had become too much of a privileged retreat for high-minded people, who enjoyed its elevated prospects, while the crude harvest of predatory life was reaped in the valleys below.

If we abstract ideal values from the body of life and cultivate them for the æsthetic or intellectual pleasure which they give, actual existence is robbed of its redemptive principle. For a time conventional morality may act as a brake upon selfish impulse. But since it has no roots in the universal and reflects little more than social expediency, it easily withers away or provokes honest realists to repudiate it. The end is an a-moral anarchy of which we have much evidence in the contemporary world.

An idealism which de-spiritualizes life by separating what is above from what is below can lead to this. But a fidelity to the actual which is blind to the ideal can be equally fatal. To become ripely human we need to outgrow the ungrounded idealism of youth, but not at the cost of abandoning the values which it too airily affirms. The spirit implants in us a vision of perfection, of the pure idea, which we are meant to embody. And it is this vision which we are required to bring into clearer and clearer focus and to vindicate through all the disillusionments by which human life puts us to the test and exposes what is false within.

As evolving creatures we are necessarily imperfect. Yet, submerged and concealed within us, is the creative infinitude which we call God. In our imperfection we are other than God, but by becoming aware of our otherness and letting go of it we can eventually overcome it. For we share the divine nature and human history has been, on the whole, such a sorry tale of strife, cruelty and misery because the majority of men have sold their divine birthright for a mess of pottage and, whatever their creeds may have been, have given rein to their imperfection instead of sedulously seeking to be "perfect even as their heavenly Father is perfect".

Christ's command "Be ye perfect" is an absolute in which the sinfulness, so much stressed by organized Christianity, needs to be swallowed up. Our reality is not what we are in our faultiness, but what we are ideally. Despite all the verbal quibblings of sophists in which we may seek to evade the simple imperatives of the spirit, we know that certain values are eternally true and necessary under all circumstances, that they are of the essence of life and, indeed, its real substance. Admittedly, if we abstract them from life in our mind, they become at best beautiful ghosts. We need to make a home for them, to take them to our hearts, to offer them the humble ground of our bodies in which they can take root and fulfil their creative task, that of spiritualizing every level of our nature, not by some perverse denial of natural instinct, but by enlightening and enlarging it.

The more proud or wilful the bent of our nature is, the harder it is to make the act of submission upon which Nina, in Tchekov's play, *The Seagull*, insists, when she says that in our work, as in our lives, what matters is not the excitement of pursuing some great aim, of cultivating lofty thoughts or impressing the world by some singular achievement. What alone really matters is "knowing how to submit to life in faith".

But within that simple phrase so much is contained. The life to which we have to learn to submit is not confined to the world of sense-perception or even of moral obligations. It is the life, too, of the visionary mind and the loving heart to which we only gain entrance when we have yielded up the outer personality which we have acquired through our upbringing and generally through our outward contact with life. So long as we slumber in this cocoon which habit has woven, our real being cannot grow. It is only by remembering that real being that we can forget ourselves.

Death, in obedience to life, is self-extinction on whatever level it occurs. To die in the body is to cease to be conscious. But to die to self in the soul is to awake to full awareness. For the spirit is then free to enter wholly into the soul and to irradiate and activate us from within. The ideal and the actual are thus brought into fruitful relationship, and by aspiring to a higher knowledge and trying to live as if we already possessed it, we attract it to us.

Until, by observing the habits of our outer self and abandoning them, we begin to live inwardly, we cannot really understand or wisely handle the outer world. We see this very clearly today when observation, as practised by physical scientists, has changed the face of the world without effecting any real change in man himself or qualifying him to use this new knowledge and its accompanying facilities for his own true good. At the same time those who are addicted to ideas and logic seldom have more real insight or control over their own inner world than those who look outward. For abstract ideas can be almost as external to real being as facts, as well as being dictated by unrecognized inner compulsions. Nor can there be any real growth so long as we indulge our minds in an ideal world beyond our own shadow, of which we need to become fully conscious.

On the other hand, to dream of a life more perfect than the one we are living need not be an indulgence. Indeed it is almost a necessity as a spur to creative effort. For we cannot expect our relation to actuality to undergo a sudden change. We have misconceived the outer world through isolating it from our inner being and only gradually can we transform our relationship to it as we liberate that being. To submit to life in faith and to see it with new eyes is the act of a free man, not of an automaton. To be free to perform such an act we have to dissociate ourselves from the mechanical routine which constitutes ordinary life and replace standardized activities by living responses. We need, in short, to imagine life, moment by moment, in the act of living it, if we are not to degrade it into a mere fact. To be imaginative is to be awake in our essence.

Few of us realize to what an extent our life consists of stock reactions, endlessly repeated. How seldom do we act purely and freely, with a full consciousness of what we are doing and of the context within which we are acting. Equally how seldom can we arrest in our minds the backwash of the events which have happened to us in the immediate or distant past. Consequently both our bodies and our minds are a field of continuous reflex action over which we have little control, since we are not sufficiently awake in ourselves to notice what is happening. To grow spiritually this thraldom to external life must be broken.

And it can only be broken as we learn to recollect ourselves in those higher centres of our being from which we are free to act creatively within life and upon it. We can then be receptive to life and to all the events in which we are involved, but with a positive understanding which is that of the spirit within us.

By maintaining this state of alert receptiveness, of loving discernment, we achieve the correct balance between positive and negative forces. And this ensures harmony and co-operation between the different levels of our being. For to be mindful is to be awake, not only in the mind, but in all the other faculties, and to disarm distraction by quiet watchfulness. Distraction may come from without, but the weakness, the lack of collectedness, is always in ourselves. The peaceful depths of the ocean are not disturbed by all the waters that flow into it. So it can be with us when we cease to cling desirously to existence and to be tossed hither and thither by its currents.

There is no alternative, then, to the task of self-discovery, of awakening to the world within, learning to conform to its laws, and allowing our nature to be cleansed and changed by its spiritual climate. Life means us to become wholly conscious of itself, to emerge from the physical darkness, in which we either serve or violate nature blindly, into the light and liberty of awareness of being. But to take sides, in the smallest degree, with light, as we conceive it, against life or, like Lucifer, to appropriate it mentally, as if it were our own to use and enjoy, is to break the creative bond between heaven and earth.

For that which is timeless and undying in us to become real we must consent in our souls to die into time. For this is how spirit descends into the substance of human life and works creatively in it. The dreaming idealist in the heaven of his own devising fails to make this descent and so cannot change himself or help the world to change. At the other extreme the materialist, who can only credit the physically measurable manifestations of life as real, denies and so makes ineffective the forces which could free his earth-bound consciousness.

Through thus misusing or rejecting the gift of consciousness within us we sin against life. And until our consciousness is corrected by what Henry James called a "total immersion in the fountain of being", our self-conscious sins against life will continue. We need faith for such an act of immersion because what we are committing ourselves to is not the life we can see and measure, but an immeasurable mystery, an absolute value which lies hidden within us and within all that is without. It is, to quote a recent writer, "that part of man that is not subject to growth or decay, but is eternally living in his heart, eternally waiting to be recognized and loved."*

To recognize and love it we need faith which opens our hearts and minds to superconscious sources of knowledge. But we need, also, to see clearly the difference between the dimension of being to which our true self belongs and the stream of impure life which we impersonate. This life has no real substance. It consists of negative thoughts, dark moods or hostile feelings, of passing excitements and elations, of vanity, self-pity, self-deception, of anger, jealousy and envy, of anxiety and impatience, and day-dreaming. Though we live in such thoughts and feelings, they are not really our own. We succumb to them as the atmosphere succumbs to depressions or a society to the prevalence of an infectious disease. At most we wear them as masks and constantly change the masks we wear under pressure from outside. Until we see them as other than ourselves, we cannot begin to discern what we really are. But when we see them as essentially unreal and as wasteful hindrances to true living and make a habit of observing, impersonally and uncritically when they are present and active in us and dissociating ourselves from them, we can

* From *The One Work* by Anne Gage.

gradually weaken the hold they have over us and dis-
courage their intrusion.

Such neutral inward vigilance, which is quite distinct
from moral self-concern, is the necessary condition of
discovering ourselves as rooted in being. The world of
being is, also, a world of thought and feeling, but not
induced or imposed from without. Just as true ideas are
creative or archetypal and come to us, when we are recollected, with power to reveal the real, so the inner states
which express our central truth are charged with wisdom,
compassion, harmony and peace. We can live in such states
if we choose, just as we can live in one place or another in
the outer world. When we have found our way into them,
we begin to share in the work of bringing heaven to earth
and raising earth to heaven. To perform this creative work
we must be free to respond to the dual rhythm of life and
death.

Out of the inexhaustible well of being in us the fountain
of life rises and falls. Rising, it lives, falling, it dies to rise
again. But most of us are loath to let it die. In our pride and
self-will, our fear or audacity, we resist the force of gravity
at the moment when we should yield to it. We try to force
life onward to some goal of our own conceiving. By so
doing we destroy its form as a fountain and change it into
a turbulent torrent in which we are either swept away or
against which we wastefully struggle.

When life is sought for itself, we endlessly pursue ends
instead of rhythmically returning to our beginning. But
life is not an end. It is a means of being, an expression of
being, and a continual return to being. To experience it as
this we need to surrender it in the act of affirming it,
resisting the fascination, which the mere force and sensation of life exercise over us, and recollecting ourselves
in the source from which the fountain springs. Then only
can it resume its play in us.

We cannot hope to break the long established momentum

of avid or anxious living all at once. To abandon the old reactions, to divest ourselves of our familiar clothes, whether pretentious or squalid, and to be naked to the embrace of reality is a daunting task, even when we are awake to the necessity of it and have had foretastes of the joy and meaning of liberation. But there are teachers who have accomplished this task and can aid us, if not in person, through their printed words. And life is the wisest teacher of all when we are humble enough to learn from her and work with her. Indeed no words of wisdom can help us unless we put them and ourselves continually to the test of life.

Thus, for example, the doctrine of "bare attention", which forms the basis of Buddhist discipline and the gateway to "right Mindfulness" needs to be practised with unobtrusive persistence in every task in which we are engaged or towards any person we may encounter or when we are withdrawn into the silence of ourselves – that silence over which usually pours a continuous traffic of mind and memory. We cannot truly attend to the object of the moment, whether it be a person, a thing, a thought or a feeling, until we cease to be a machine running on the fuel supplied by life from without and reacting tensely or blindly to the stimuli provided by external contacts. The practice of "bare attention" trains us, not only to concentrate fully on one thing at a time, but to be recollected in ourselves in the act of experiencing.

To see natural life for what it is, when unillumined from within, and to maintain this vision of it by constant recollection, is to break the Circean spell with which it binds us. That is why Gautama named "right views" as the first step of his "noble eightfold path" and why Buddhism has emphasized so strongly, too strongly, perhaps, at times, the importance of analyzing our emotions and of calm, collected thinking as a means to liberation.

To many warm-hearted people the effort to experience

life without personal reaction may seem bound to kill the nerve of feeling, without which relationship would be as cold as a mathematical equation. But in fact we cannot share true feeling or understanding with another, until our minds are emptied of the desire and aversion or the wilful impetuosity which too often distract and confuse them. Only then can we join in the dance of life, that dance which the mystic, Henri Suso, described as "a heavenly flowing forth and back again into the lovely abyss of the divine mystery".

For the life-impulse should flow unimpeded into our heart from the unconscious depths in which our being is rooted. There it should meet and be irradiated by the clear light of consciousness which descends through the higher mind from the ideal plane. We prevent this organic union of life and light from developing in us by fastening on one or other of the three centres through which we live in the body, the instinctive, the emotional and the intellectual, and blindly identifying ourselves with it. Of these the instinctive motor-centre which governs muscular movement is the most mechanical and perhaps the most abused today. When we lose ourselves in it, we become the slaves of meaningless movement and cannot rest. The centres in which we feel and think are of a more subtle substance and for that reason are the more easily deranged. By living compulsively in either of them or both we morbidly excite and exaggerate their activity.

But if by detachment and recollection of our true being we cease to interfere with their natural functioning and at the same time subject them to the direction of a higher will and consciousness, the three centres will come eventually to work together as one, with perfect economy. No longer will life involve us in a continual expense of spirit through our blind subjection to it, or, as Shakespeare called it, through "lust in action". And in the peace that ensues we shall begin to experience a quite new feeling of what intrinsically we are, releasing in us new and finer resources of energy and understanding, and freeing us from the psychological complexes which have crippled our capacity both to love and to know.

3

To immerse ourselves, then, in the fountain of being involves a sustained reversal of all our usual habits and of the way we have reacted to life. Previously, in fact, our interest in life has been focused in self-interest. We have generally valued it in the degree that it pleased us or enhanced our self-importance. And we have resented or defied it when it hurt or humiliated us. If an awareness of being, rhythmic and harmonious, is now to replace the confusion and conflict or the mechanical uniformity of self-centred living, we must now abandon this offensive or defensive relation to life with its private passions and preferences.

We cannot come close to life or experience it intimately unless we are free both to give ourselves to it and to receive in full awareness all it has to give from moment to moment. When we are no longer intoxicated either by ideas or emotions or prejudiced by any form of self-concern, death and life can fulfil their interplay in us and the eternal can commune through us with time. If we crave for the eternal directly or exclusively, we discredit time, despite the fact that religious literature is full of such impassioned longings and cries of hunger and thirst.

Such cries are natural to our human condition when we are most eager to escape from its disabilities or from the anguish which time can seem so inexorably to lay upon us. But if our lives are truly to unfold their destined pattern, we must wait and watch for the moment, the hour, the day which are timely and intended. What is of eternal value can only come to us through the ministry and mediation of time, while time quite disjoined from the timeless, if that were possible, would be but a handful of sand trickling through fingers that cannot hold it.

Today, in a world of reactive haste and hurry, the temptation to spurn the *tempo* in which life can be fully experienced is overwhelming. And the consequences of being forced to work against time are all around us in unrest and violence or simply in superficial and shoddy achievement. Even more dangerously is it shown in the way technical capacity has outrun the moral insight needed to control and direct if. For individuals and communities need time for balanced growth and greed and fear deprive them of this.

Certainly, if in looking back upon our lives, the results are not altogether barren, if the years have something to show beyond wasted endeavour or ephemeral achievement, it is because we have allowed time to discipline us, to retard our fevered impulse, and to teach us the patience and humility without which nothing of lasting worth can be done. The blessing of the timeless has to be earned. Spiritually and humanly we have to "serve our time". We are apprentices in the craft of living who aspire to be Master artists. In learning our craft we need always the inspiration which comes to us from beyond time, just as we need always to be venturing into the unknown space within ourselves. But for the unknown to be made perceptible and for the wordless idea to find its predestined form, the ministry of time, which enables us to work things out by degrees, is essential.

Time is the great craftsman of the timeless, a teacher, too, that can fructify all that we potentially are and have in us to do. For to learn from time is to grow in time. It prepares the ground in our bodies and souls in which the seed of transformation that is sown from above, or from beyond time, can germinate. Imperceptibly it helps us to ripen, releasing us, little by little, from that world of self-centred illusion which is not of time's making, but of our own. It is no use pursuing reality into the distance in the hope that we may capture it beyond the horizon and bring it back as a trophy, gloriously won. Unless we find it here and now in this small, difficult corner of earth that asks for our service and our concern, we shall never truly find it at all. For "what little beauty and peace is to be found in the societies of men", as Tagore wrote, "is owing to the daily performance of small duties, not to big doings and fine talk".

Disillusionment is one of the means by which time tests the validity of our dreams. For though imagination is a god-given faculty without which creation is impossible, we can easily allow it to spin for us a pervasive web of fiction, in which to escape from the drabness of fact or the discomfort of facing and changing ourselves. Such fiction varies in quality from sentimental or ingenious fantasy to the more responsible imaginings in which some effort is made to relate the dream to the fact. Time is necessary to develop and deepen this relationship in ourselves and to shock us into awareness of the resistance of matter to our dreams and the limits which we must accept.

But it is not only our ideal impulses which need to be tested and purified. Our one-sided instinct for life is, perhaps, the greatest hindrance which we have to overcome. For until our belief in life no longer involves a recoil from death, until we know that life by itself can never satisfy the soul's deepest needs, but only a life informed and renewed from beyond its earthly limits, our life will remain a tomb from the entrance of which the stone has yet to be rolled away. This, surely, is the real meaning of the "empty tomb" in the Gospel and of the words of the two men in shining garments who said: "Why seek ye the living among the dead? He is not here, but is risen." To be re-born through faith into the greater life, we must needs abandon our belief in the power of death to annul it.

Thus it is that of all the gifts of time the most precious is the persistent reminder it offers us that death is a condition of life. Creation requires death for the birth of life and if, as spiritual beings, we are deathless, this does not qualify us to look down upon an earthly world, subject to death, from a spiritual eminence which is no more than an ideal of the mind.

But by consenting to die to all that separates us from life we allow the spiritual light to descend from its higher levels and enter the womb of darkness in which the soul awaits its quickening touch. For long the soul reflects only the life of the outer world. At birth it clothes itself in a physical body in which it suffers pleasure and pain through the physical senses. It thus shares the body's craving for life and hostility to death. And so long as it clings to its bodily vehicle it cannot be spiritually quickened. To receive the light, it has to turn inward and reflect, not the outer world that is always under sentence of death, but the inner world of the pure, undying Self. By thus forestalling the moment of physical death it awakens to the reality of its immortal being. No longer dependent for its knowledge on bodily sensation, it draws its insight directly from the divine sun of which it is a ray. The child of this union of spirit and soul is the new man, the real individual, in whom the feud between self-consciousness and life is resolved and who is free, therefore, to doff all the multiple masks of personality and to be wholly himself.

The older we grow the more capable should we be of thus dying into a new life by ceasing to identify ourselves, either positively or negatively, with the moods of the body. Age can, indeed, increasingly remind us of our physical helplessness. But if we do not resent the handicaps it imposes, this can prove an aid to deeper participation. For the less we are able to impose our personal will upon life, the freer we are to discover a will within us that is much more truly ours through being universal in origin. By this will we can act or refrain from action with an inner freedom from all external compulsions. Thus helplessness, if rightly accepted, can teach us how to receive help from beyond the natural world and its disabilities.

Death, to the partial vision of the natural man, is the enemy which has to be fought, though it can never be defeated, only held at bay or forced back into the shadows where it belongs. But our energy drains away in this wilful warfare. For, in resisting death, we are opposing life. The animal wholly affirms life in his instinctive struggle for survival. But when this struggle is transferred to the mental and moral plane, it becomes a deathly attempt to perpetuate the divided self. The consequences of such an attempt are so painful and, if persisted in, so disastrous, that eventually we are compelled to abandon it.

And as we no longer clutch at life through a fear of death, we begin to recover consciously something of the care-free spontaneity of our youth. Once again we taste the freedom to Be, which results from a complete readiness not to be. The happily young, like the happily old, do not cling to life and so death does not cling to them but opens a way into infinity. When this dual infinity of life and death, as Rilke called it, is denied by us, we are continually conscious of finite hazards and threatened by apparent destruction. Death, in its endlessly beneficent task of dissolution for re-creation, no longer nourishes our life and ministers to what is eternal in us. Instead it haunts our imagination as a pitiless devourer which, indeed, it is in its merely temporal aspect.

The essential meaning of our existence on earth is the resolving of this delusive feud between life and death which we maintain within us and project into all we do. Until it is resolved, we are doomed to spiritual impotence, like lovers who should recoil from the total embrace in which they at once fear and desire to consummate their passion.

Our ordinary life may, indeed, be regarded as a long illness, dangerous and ultimately, if nothing is done about it, fatal, but from which we can, if we turn to the light within and cleanse our hearts to receive it, find ourselves eventually, not only convalescent, but blessed with an inward health that no circumstances can undermine. For the light leads us into the spiritual world and the more real the life of that world is to us, the less do we fear the loss of physical life, until ultimately fear is consumed in an ever-present awareness of Being and survives, if at all, only as a reflex action of the body.

We are, then, in communion with death, as with a lover or friend or, to change the metaphor for a more impersonal one, we are happily immersed in the great maternal deep in which our springs of life are continually renewed, as in the nightly ritual of sleep. But before that at-onement can be consummated, tenacious mental habits must be reversed, short-sighted hopes and desires abandoned, all the false things that have to die before the true death can live in us and be loved. And this is something which, for the most part, only time can teach us, as much by what it withholds as by what it gives.

For dying is an art, which has to be learned in the practice of life by allowing it to dissolve our assertive will and refine our perceptions, until we come to feel habitually the mystery of death in each new-born moment and to see with wonder in all around us that mutual embrace of light and shadow, of idea and substance in which life and death unite. This is the art to which those who are growing old should in particular devote themselves, thus helping to form the new body or bodies within them in which they are soon to live. Yet an assent to death is as much a grace of ardent youth, though unconscious then, as it is of an old age fulfilled in wisdom and understanding. In fact the whole of our life, with its physical and mental changes and its continual demands upon us to adapt to new circumstances and pressures from within and without, is a testing of our capacity to maintain and consciously deepen the union between living and dying by which we are created and can ourselves create.

The fruitful interplay of all the opposites which meet in our nature depends on our finding the middle, neutral point between them. Of these the primal opposites are heaven and earth, the inner and the outer worlds which, in traditional Christianity, have been named the supernatural and the natural orders. There is no real conflict between these two orders despite the tendency of most religions to range them against each other. Indeed Jesus declared in one of the apocryphal sayings attributed to him that his kingdom would not come until "two shall be one, and the without as the within, and the male with the female, neither male nor female".

The supernatural and natural worlds belong to different levels of experience, but there is a correspondence between them and the higher is present in the lower. It is true that so long as we are divided in ourselves and deny our inner light in indulging our instinct for life, we have to work against what is generally assumed to be natural, but which is a distortion of nature. Only so can we recover our true spiritual centre.

But to spiritualize life is not to deny it nor need we repudiate instinct in striving to affirm a higher faculty. Our task is to transform natural life from within by the light of a new and true order of ideas given to us from a more interior level of our being. In the words of Frédéric Amiel, "divine life is a series of successive deaths, in which the spirit throws off its imperfections and symbols and yields to the growing attraction of that ineffable centre of gravitation, the sun of intelligence and love."*

The real inner world, if we can find our way into it and make it our centre of gravity, is super-natural because

* Quoted by Édouard Schuré in *The Great Initiates*.

in it we are not enslaved by necessity as all other natural creatures are. In the spiritual world the ineluctable law of Karma, of cause and effect, of sin and punishment, is modified and ultimately overruled by the informing power of "Grace" and of love. It is thus a world of true freedom – the freedom to understand and to forgive. For heaven, as William Blake said, is a state of perpetual forgiveness. Only when we have entered this dimension of being can we become truly conscious of That which creates and transcends all life, including our own.

That such consciousness is possible while we are still a part of natural life shows that the two orders are not insuperably divided or opposed. If they were, That which includes both in its total Being would be divided against itself. For this reason we cannot fully experience life spiritually, if, in the slightest degree, we recoil from the natural order. Nor can we fully enjoy the gift of natural life until we experience it as a supernatural grace. The riches of nature, as Traherne wrote, "are our souls and bodies, with all their faculties, senses, and endowments", so wonderfully made to "enjoy the world aright", to be at one with the sea flowing in our veins and to be "clothed with the heavens, and crowned with the stars".

But this cannot be, so long as we live exclusively on the level of nature, conscious only of the body of life and impotently involved in it. To extend our physical consciousness is but to enlarge the field of our essential ignorance, whether it be by adding to our knowledge of the processes of the physical world or of our own vital and mental selves. Really to know, we have also to be. And this involves transferring our consciousness from the circumference of the personal self to our spiritual centre. By this transference nature in us is enlightened and consecrated from within and what had become deathly in it, through separation from its supernatural source, is redeemed.

Natural death can then become an expression of

supernatural life and we can cry with the voice of a lover whose eyes are opened to the hidden beauty in the heart of death, "oh death, where is thy sting?" – a lover who cannot praise life without praising death too and in whom the joy of life fulfils itself in the act of giving life away.

In the natural order the body dies that life may renew itself in another form. In the supernatural order the self dies that the light may reveal itself in a liberated soul. By clinging to the natural order, even when we resent its sway, we impose on the soul the mortality of the body and rob it of its essential freedom. But the quickened soul cannot die. It can only suffer and endure in those who are too self-conscious to sleep the sleep of the natural life, but have yet to open to the Light that is Consciousness itself. In this state we are torn between death and life; we earn "the wages of sin". All the negative impulses to which we yield are the outcome of our failure to maintain the creative balance between life and death as we ascend from the bondage of natural life towards the liberating knowledge of spiritual being.

But sin did not bring death into the world. It came between death and life and poisoned their relation. Love re-unites them. It restores the balance, not by triumphing over the death which is essential to life, but by expressing in its pure soul the eternal mystery by which we can die, moment by moment, to separation to be re-born in the Whole. In the fruition of love life and death are at one. For love accepts death gladly, not in a pious hope of some future resurrection, but in the knowledge that death is birth on every level of life and that in every act and thought in which we willingly die, eternity breaks into time and earth communes with heaven.

The author of "The Revelation of St John The Divine" saw "in the midst of the Throne a Lamb, as it had been slain". In his vision the Throne symbolizes the divine power and sovereignty and the Lamb, standing in the midst of it, is the sacrificial love in the heart of creation, which, by truly suffering death, reaches down to the depths of life and endlessly transforms the darkness into light. That is the mystery which each of us is called to fathom as we struggle to become fully conscious of What and who we are.

Epilogue

Man is not at home as a creature of earth even when he seems to be most earth-bound. He is in essence a spiritual being, that is a being whose real nature is not determined by the physical body in which it is lodged or the physical context which seems for so long to restrict and condition it. He may, indeed, become so absorbed in the outer world and its alluring objects as almost to forget the subject that he is. But his descent into matter has no meaning unless it helps to quicken and enrich his subjective experience of life and unless it acts as a fulcrum by which the consciousness of his real being is awakened, enabling him to find his spiritual feet in the physical world. Otherwise he will be deluded by what St John called "the vain-glory of life" or broken by the treachery of existence, which flatters hope only to betray it.

Modern man, despite his boasted technical triumphs over the physical world, is in danger of losing his spiritual footing in the world. He is lamentably poor in what a wise doctor, Vladimir Lindenberg, has called "the endothymic substances, namely the bonds of religion and the inner security they bring, love, a sense of awe, a feeling of responsibility, humility, inner stability, a readiness to suffer or to be joyful and a feeling of being at one with the cosmos and its creatures."*

To recover his spiritual footing and thereby to find both

* *Meditation and Mankind* by Vladimir Lindenberg.

[220]

inner freedom and real community with his fellows, man must regain contact, as I have tried to show in this book, with the silence within and beyond himself. The hideous and ever-increasing noise of the modern world proclaims his attachment to the transitory. To regain the silence without which sound is a coarse affront to sensibility a man must turn inward in search of the world of being which underlies his outer existence, and in which consciousness originates and is unconditioned.

Consciousness is not necessary to existence which is maintained by its own vital momentum. As mere creatures of existence we are in bondage to life and such self-consciousness as we have is imposed on us by life and our varying reactions to it. We imagine that our thoughts are free and our own. But, in fact, they are determined by forces stored up in the subconscious depths of our human past, channelled by our ancestry, modified by our environment and vitalized by our attachment to the life of instinct and the senses.

But in time we become conscious of this bondage. We recognize how little we are independent of the stream of ever-changing phenomena in which we are immersed and with which we identify ourselves. Whether physically in our movements from place to place or psychically in our fluctuating moods and states of mind, we are the puppets of a complicated past which repeats itself in the present and will continue to repeat itself, unless we can dissociate ourselves from its unconscious mechanism. To do this we have to work purposefully on ourselves and the more steadfastly we see how little real identity we ordinarily possess and how subject we are to the play of negative or conflicting forces, the more convinced we become that within us is a principle of freedom which can deliver us from the blind mechanism of outer life.

This principle is inherent in pure Mind which is not dependent upon sensations, but shines by its own light.

As, through detachment, we succeed in cleansing and tranquillizing our nature, this light begins to shine through those higher centres in us which could not become active until we had put the lower rooms of our house in order. This light reveals to us a world of inner Reality to which our spiritual being belongs and which is informed by a truth that transcends the limits of our earth-bound faculties. Those who succeed in rising to this level in themselves are freed from servitude to life and its subconscious forces and can act creatively.

The subconscious in us can thus be regarded as the past from which only the superconscious can free us. And our task in the present is to transform our natural life by drawing down into it the light and dynamism of this higher consciousness. Then, instead of the past continuing to determine our future by the blind working of cause and effect, the enlightened future to which we inwardly open begins to re-create our past in its true pattern. For the whole of our past is in us now and can blossom anew in the present, if we can see it differently and redeem its errors by a new power of insight and the forgiveness which such insight dictates.

To feel and eventually to know that it is possible thus to change ourselves and our relationship to life from within destroys, in the only way it can be destroyed, the sense of impotence and dread which the contemporary man-made world can hardly fail to induce in any sensitive soul. Seeing this outer world from a new depth within ourselves we realize how little even the worst that man in his blindness can do can affect the unassailable reality of what we are. "Assured in the dark tides of the world at rest," we can echo Rupert Brooke's words, "Who is so safe as we?"

But in this safety is no smugness or complacency and no fastidious withdrawal from the agonies of a world in travail. To rise above the bondage of life is not to reject it nor the lessons which it can teach us, but to be free to live with

open eyes and tranquil hearts and a fullness of understanding which only the informing light of consciousness
can give. It is this light which we seek when we undertake
the great task of changing ourselves and so of changing, if
only to a minute degree, the quality and conditions of life
on this planet. The spiritual atmosphere in which humanity
lives is poisoned by dark thoughts and must be cleansed
before heaven can fully enter into earth and redeem it. And
it is in the inner nature of each one of us that the cleansing
must begin. "No pills, no short-wave treatment," as Dr
Lindenberg has written, "no sects, no reform movements
can help. There is only one possibility – to uncover step by
step the buried way to the spirit, cautiously and with infinite patience groping through the dark."

And even when the darkness lifts, we cannot know the
spirit as we know the contorted self which we suppose ourselves to be. The spirit "bloweth where it listeth" and all
the talent for definition upon which the intellect prides
itself is powerless to pin down its ineffable reality or
measure the joy of being born through it into a new life.
But as we learn to watch and disown the false personality
which masquerades as ourselves, this imposter gradually
loses the force and vitality which we have lent it. And the
more deflated it becomes, the more space is there within
us which the spirit can fill. In Boehme's words, "there
where before will was, there now is nothing and where
nothing is, there is God's love alone effective."

It is only then that we see the meaning of the Zen Master's
question, "What are your original features which you have
even prior to your birth?" For we are increasingly conscious
of the mystery of being in which we and all life are immersed and in the heart of which the real and constant "I"
of each one of us originates. As when the work of some old
Master is brought to light by the removal of what has
been superimposed upon it, so the image of us conceived
in the divine Mind is slowly recovered by the dissolution

of the plausible self-portrait which we have drawn through a predisposition to fear or pride or vanity.

In this book I have tried to suggest some of the ways in which that work of restoration may be initiated and carried forward. This work is in no way destructive of the pigment of life. Indeed it requires a sensitiveness to that pigment, to the body of the natural world in which the spirit clothes itself, and the natural faculties through which it transmits its light and love, a sensitiveness which the materialist, however intellectually acute, so sadly lacks. To those who see "the jewel in the heart of the lotus" all life is inexpressibly dear and precious, even when its purpose is thwarted and its beauty marred. The spirit, when it flowers in man, has a concern not for power or gain or self-display, but for life itself. It alone can counter the brutalizing effects of the machine on modern man. It alone can lead man home to what is real in himself. Of that return an Eastern teacher has written:

Like a man who was absent from home a long time and does not know on his return what to do first, so glad is he, just so the spirit when it is united with the soul, is filled with an inexpressible joy and gladness.

We are all prodigals, feeding on the husks of applied science, until we return to share that joy together.

Photoset and printed by photo-lithography in Great Britain by William Clowes and Sons Ltd., London and Beccles

63 Kamayoqs

37 july datum